Camp Cook's Companion
A Ragged Mountain Press Pocket Guide

Alan S. Kesselheim

Ragged Mountain Press / McGraw-Hill
Camden, Maine • New York • Chicago • San Francisco • Lisbon •
London • Madrid • Mexico City • Milan • New Delhi • San Juan •
Seoul• Singapore • Sydney • Toronto

Look for these other Ragged Mountain Press Pocket Guides:

Backpacker's Pocket Guide, Chris Townsend
Edible Wild Plants and Herbs, Alan M. Cvancara
Sea Kayaker's Pocket Guide, Shelley Johnson
Wilderness First Aid, Paul G. Gill Jr., M.D.

Ragged Mountain Press
A Division of The **McGraw-Hill** Companies

10 9 8 7 6 5 4 3 2 1
Copyright © 2002 Ragged Mountain Press
All rights reserved. The publisher takes no responsibility for the use of any of the materials or methods described in this book, nor for the products thereof. The name "Ragged Mountain Press" and the Ragged Mountain Press logo are trademarks of The McGraw-Hill Companies. Printed in the United States of America.

Acknowledgments for previously published material appear on page 137, which constitutes a continuation of the copyright page.

ISBN 0-07-138801-X
Library of Congress Cataloging-in-Publication information is not available for this title.

Questions regarding the content of this book should be addressed to
Ragged Mountain Press
P.O. Box 220
Camden, ME 04843
www.raggedmountainpress.com

Questions regarding the ordering of this book should be addressed to
The McGraw-Hill Companies
Customer Service Department
P.O. Box 547
Blacklick, OH 43004
Retail customers: 1-800-262-4729
Bookstores: 1-800-722-4726

This book is printed on 60# Thor White Antique by R. R. Donnelley
Design by Carol Gillette
Page layout by Shannon Swanson
Production management by Janet Robbins
Edited by Jonathan Eaton and Lisa Perkins

All photographs by Alan S. Kesselheim or Marypat Zitzer

Contents

Introduction

Let's be honest. Writers of cookbooks are thieves. They prefer to call themselves "recipe collectors," but what they're really up to is little more than boldfaced robbery. They "collect" recipes from their families, neighbors, and trip partners, from dinner parties and other recipe collections. Grandma's Sunday dinner, Uncle Jim's favorite biscuit dough, an old college roommate's casserole are all fair game. We add different spices, change an ingredient, call it something else, and suddenly it's our own recipe.

This collection is no exception. In fact, this book makes a blatant point of cribbing—but only from the best (and always with permission!). I've culled the finest meals in top-drawer outdoor cookbooks for you: *The Winter Wilderness Companion* by Garrett Conover and Alexandra Conover; *The One-Burner Gourmet* by Harriett Barker; *The One Pan Gourmet* by Don Jacobson; *Cruising Cuisine* by Kay Pastorius; *Kids Outdoors* by Victoria Logue, Frank Logue, and Mark Carroll; *The Portable Baker* by Jean Spangenberg and Samuel Spangenberg; *The Outdoor Dutch Oven Cookbook* by Sheila Mills; and *Trail Food* by yours truly, Alan Kesselheim (see acknowledgments on page 137). We've standardized abbreviations and terms, but otherwise the recipes reflect the flavor, as it were, of the authors. So, for example, some recipes give home oven temperatures for advance preparation, and others don't; some indicate in the ingredients list everything down to the fat needed to grease the pan, and others don't. But all these recipes have stood up to years of use by readers just like you.

Brand new to print are a clutch of original Kesselheim recipes—you can identify them because they don't have a source indicated at the end of the recipe. Actually, many of my own tried-and-true trail recipes are the result of decades of backcountry pilfering. Time to fess up and thank the silent contributors: Kim Blommel, Charlie Crangle, Dorcas Miller, Craig Kesselheim, Kris Carrillo, Marypat Zitzer, Grant Herman, among many other camp partners whose meals have sustained and inspired me in the wilderness and whose ideas are behind many of my tastiest recipes.

The book's table of contents provides a general guide to categories, and the index pinpoints specific foods and meals. Plus, each chapter has a handy list of recipes right up front for quick reference. This book is meant to be taken along and propped open alongside rivers, in crannies of mountain talus, under Arctic skies, and on desert slickrock. My fondest hope is that your copy will look field-worn, bug-stained, rain-weathered, and food-spattered in short order.

Some recipes are best made in advance, before you leave home—energy bars (page 64), granola (page 35), or jerky (page 66), for example. Others can be prepackaged with measured and combined ingredients to make cooking in the field more convenient. (See Conversions and Equivalents, beginning on page 135, for help if you're more comfortable cooking in metric units or for information on the measurement abbreviations used in this book.)

By all means, feel free to tweak recipes to your liking. Add stuff, substitute fresh food for dehydrated or the other way around, play with ingredients and seasonings—make each recipe yours. That's certainly what I did!

Camp Cooking

NUTRITION OUTDOORS

The backcountry is no place to be dieting, skimping, cutting corners, or otherwise playing fast and loose with nutritional needs. Our increasingly sedentary lifestyle makes the wilderness one of the few places left where we can indulge our appetite without guilt and even feel wholesomely justified about three good, sizable meals a day, plus a snack or two.

Backpacking, skiing, paddling, biking, and other recreations require fuel; it's as simple as that. Without adequate food to keep us going, outdoor activities are a strain at best, and downright risky at worst. Properly fueled, our bodies thrive outdoors, where there is no need for fitness-club workouts, lap swimming, or weight machines. The demands of the daily routine keep us fit and trim and prime our appetite appropriately.

When prompted by steady physical activity rather than work-life stress and neuroses, hunger tends to kick in free of compulsion and other eating dysfunction. On the trail the combination of activity, travel challenges, and group camaraderie put food and appetite in healthy perspective.

Food may also be the most underrated component of successful outdoor trips. Attention usually focuses on the training regimen, skills enhancement, group dynamics, cutting-edge gear, and itinerary. But when the food is insufficient, boring, or uninspired, everything else—from physical performance to trip morale—goes flat. Pretty soon the group conversation centers on getting back home and on the elaborate, indulgent menu waiting somewhere else. In fact, however, there's no reason you can't enjoy cooking fantasies and luxurious meals in the outdoors. Turns out it's the best place of all to indulge.

Outdoor nutrition should be balanced, steady, rich with variety, and filling. When it is, those wistful fireside conversations about the food back home evaporate. Backcountry fare can also be reasonably priced and easy to fix, without having to go the boil-a-bag route.

It's important to recognize that each of us comes equipped with different engines, not to mention different tastes and preferences. Body size, percentage of fat in our physical make-up, and metabolic rates all affect the need for food. You're the best judge of your own dietary idiosyncrasies and your own outdoor comfort and safety needs. Pay attention to your body and don't be self-conscious about adjusting menus and amounts per your individual requirements.

On the most basic level, all else being equal, the 200-pound (91 kg) hiker will need a third more food than their 120-pound (54 kg) partner. In addition to body size, activity level and environmental conditions make a huge difference. What is plenty of food on a sunny, 70°F (21°C) saunter would be skimpy indeed on a winter camping outing or when the wind is blowing sleet sideways on an exposed ridge. Extraordinary conditions, either in terms of weather or physical challenge, can easily double a person's metabolic needs.

We have, and for good reason, become increasingly conscious of fat in our diets. Our backcountry food, however, should have an adequate balance of fat, protein, and carbohydrates. In particular, fat provides the most efficient source of insulation against cold, lubricates the joints, and cushions internal organs. Nutritional experts generally agree that a blend of 20 percent fats (dairy, peanut butter, oils, and nuts and seeds), 60 percent carbohydrates (sugar, fruit, veggies, and cereals), and 20 percent protein (meat, dairy, fish, grains, and legumes) is a healthy balance when we're engaged in outdoor activities.

Again, the wilderness is not the place to limit calories. It's the one place where we not only can *get away with* having a fair percentage of fat in our food, but where we actually *need* it—especially when the going gets difficult and the conditions become challenging.

With a little planning and some great recipes, you need no longer feel you're enduring a gastronomic endurance test in exchange for a dose of outdoor exhilaration. Instead, your wilderness immersions will acquire a rewarding and satisfying culinary dimension.

THE COST-AND-LABOR EQUATION

The old adage "you get what you pay for" is stood on its head when it comes to buying food for outdoor trips: the most expensive option gets you the least—while the cheapest gets you the most—nutritious and satisfying fare. However, you do get what you work for. The most laborious food strategy yields the best menu, while the easy way out results in the worst food.

In other words, if you buy prepackaged camp food from an outdoor retailer, you'll spend a heap of change and save yourself some pretrip sweat, but you'll eat poorly on the trail. Buy fresh food, or better yet, grow your own, dehydrate and package it yourself, and you'll eat as well in the boonies as you ever will at home.

GREATEST EXPENSE AND LEAST LABOR

Prepackaged camp food has come a long way. In the early days, a few decades ago, much of it was very nearly inedible. People choked it down in the field only because they had to have fuel, any fuel. Contemporary products feature haute cuisine entrées, flavorful spices, fancy desserts, and baked goods. What hasn't changed, however, is that all that prep, packaging, and preservative technology results in a hefty price tag, the portions tend to be on the skimpy side (at least if you're the 200-pound member of the team), and the taste, with rare exceptions, still doesn't approach anything like a home-cooked meal.

What remains seductive about this stuff is that it is incredibly easy to deal with. You just hand over your credit card, throw the food in your pack, and most of it cooks in a matter of minutes. Despite its armorlike packaging—which has the advantage that it doesn't even require dirtying pots—this type of camp food tends to be the lightest on the load.

If money isn't an object, it's worth sprinkling a few pack-

aged meals into the menu. When the weather turns nasty or you're trail weary at dinnertime, having that three-minute meal on hand is a godsend.

THE MIDDLE GROUND

Mainstream food companies have figured out that quick, lightweight, prepackaged meals are in demand. They've responded with a variety of foods—from instant hot cereal packets to easy-to-prepare entrées to no-bake desserts—that fill the same niche as the specialty camp food offerings, but do so more affordably. Health-food grocers also carry a number of organic and specialty foods from lemon couscous to spicy refried beans.

You'll probably tweak the dishes a bit, judiciously add some fresh ingredients for texture, flavorings for interest, or another dish for balance, but these days you can do pretty well outfitting your trip pantry from the grocery store aisles.

Beware, however, of additives in packaged foods. Some of the chemicals in ingredients lists are daunting, and just reading what an entrée's sodium content is can be heart-constricting.

CHEAP AND LABORIOUS

As you would expect, homemade is the best choice for trip food. Fresh food, when you can get away with hauling it (as you often can on river trips, for instance), allows a menu such as you'd expect at home. Fresh food preserved in your own food dehydrator and packaged into meals grants you lightweight, low-volume supplies even for an extended expedition (see page 13). It gets reincarnated along the trail into nutritious and creative meals that would taste pretty good anywhere.

By buying food in bulk, doing your own dehydrating, and packaging simply, you'll cut expenses by quantum leaps, reduce excess garbage, and fuel your trip engines with wholesome food that caters to your personal tastes.

The price tag is your own labor. You'll be working the dehydrator shift for days before a long trip, making forays to the grocer and farmer's market, processing and packaging your food—all part of working to earn your rations.

THE COMPROMISE POSITION

My trip equation tends to balance the options. I strive to produce the bulk of trip food from fresh supplies dehydrated at home, but I'll also throw in store-bought supplies, some fresh bulk ingredients, and a few indulgences. The mix depends on how much time I have available, how healthy my bank account is, and what the trip logistics demand.

Over the years, however, I've been so pampered with good food on the trail that I almost never succumb to a diet consisting solely of store-packaged outdoor fare. It isn't worth the expense, and more important, it isn't worth the gastronomic disappointment: I know how much better meals in the backcountry can be.

DRY YOUR OWN

Some of the recipes in *Camp Cook's Companion* call for dehydrated foods. You can certainly substitute fresh ingredients, or purchase dried or freeze-dried supplies, but if you're committed to spending fair stretches of time in the backcountry, drying your own food makes a great deal of sense.

WHY DRY?

The rationale for dehydrating your own backcountry food rests on several compelling arguments.

1. Economy: by purchasing supplies in bulk, on sale, in season, or by using garden produce, you cut your costs by a huge percentage.

2. Weight and bulk: since anywhere from 50 to 90 percent of most food is water, drying it translates to tremendous reductions in both overall weight and bulk of trip supplies.

3. Preservation: properly stored, most dried food will keep for months or years, without additives, preservatives, or other chemicals.

4. Quality control: you can dictate the source of your food, the portions in your meals, and the freshness of supplies, and then generate customized meals based on your ingredients.

EQUIPMENT

Dehydrator: You can play around with sun-drying, oven-drying, or, if you're an industrious type, building your own dryer, but far and away the most efficient and convenient course is to purchase a dehydrator. For somewhere between $40 and $300 you can buy a dependable and well-designed unit that will start paying for itself with the first load of food.

Leaving food to dry in the sun works fine as a drying method—we've done it since the beginning of time. But a commercial dehydrator does the job conveniently and safely by providing a controlled environment with optimum airflow and temperature, regardless of the weather or the season.

Look for the following features in a dryer.

- round design (best air flow and heat distribution)
- thermostatic heat control
- electric fan
- expandable capacity (usually by adding trays)
- convenient accessories—solid trays for liquids, screen inserts, jerky and yogurt makers, etc.

Food processor or blender: You can get by with a simple paring knife for prepping most foods, but a blender is handy, and a food processor really cuts prep time dramatically. Even one of those old-style Veg-o-Matic gizmos is a big help.

Storage containers: see under Storage on page 16.

Scale: A scale that measures ounces (grams) for smaller items and goes up to 25 pounds (11 kg) or so is useful for weighing out portions.

Plastic bags and labels: I usually make do with reclosable plastic bags, but you can get fancy with vacuum-sealed, heat-sealed bags if you wish. Label food with the date as you store it, so you can use supplies with the most shelf time first.

INSTRUCTIONS

Most dehydrators come with a user's manual and a pamphlet explaining basics such as drying times, food prep, and optimal temperatures. From there it's largely a matter of common sense and experience. For a more in-depth treatment of drying foods for backcountry use, pick up a copy of my *Trail Food: Drying and Cooking Food for Backpackers and Paddlers*.

FOODS TO DRY

Fruits and vegetables: These are the most common foods to dry. Some of the tougher vegetables, like carrots or broccoli, need blanching or other cooking, but softer vegetables and most fruits can be sliced and loaded directly onto the drying trays. It's best to start with fresh foods, but I've also dried many different frozen and canned foods with good results. Most fruits and vegetables are dried at temperatures of 120 to 135°F (49–57°C). Times vary greatly depending on the foods, size of pieces, and local climate.

Liquids: Sauces, fruit leathers, salsa, canned tomato sauce, refried bean paste, and eggs (see next paragraph) can also be dried with great results. Use solid trays, or solid inserts, spread the liquid or paste evenly, and dry. You can even dehydrate complete dinners, like stews or chilis, on solid trays, and then reconstitute the entire meal in the field.

Meat and dairy: Jerky, stew meat, poultry, cheeses, and eggs can all be successfully dried at home (spread liquidy foods such as sour cream, cottage cheese, and eggs on solid trays for drying). Meat and dairy are the most problematic foods to dry, however, because they tend to have a fairly high fat content and can go rancid if stored improperly or over too long a period. Foods in this group should be dried at relatively high heat (140–145°F/60–63°C) and stored for a relatively short time before use (more than two to three months is pushing it). The best storage strategy is to keep these foods in the freezer at home after they've been dried, taking them out right before you leave for the backcountry. Also, package them in single-serving amounts so that if a batch does go bad, it won't ruin a large quantity. Meats should be cooked before being dried, with the exception of jerky, which is cooked in the drying process. Dried, grated cheeses can

DRIED EGGS

After you've cleaned up a few squashed eggs in your backpack, you'll be even more tempted to take dry eggs rather than fresh next time.

To dry eggs, lightly beat 6 to 8 eggs, adding seasonings if you'd like, and pour the uncooked liquid onto a solid tray. Dry until all moisture is gone, and then crumble by hand (inside a bag) or powder in a blender. Reconstitute with $1/4$ cup water per egg.

generally be added as is to recipes, melting in the heating or cooking process. See the accompanying sidebar for instructions on drying eggs.

Grains and beans: You can reduce the cooking time of many staples by cooking and then drying them in a dehydrator. This works well for rice, dried beans, pasta, etc., and generally reduces cooking time in the field by about half.

STORAGE

The enemies of dried food are sunlight, air, moisture, and high temperatures. The ideal storage site, therefore, is cool, dark, and dry. Airtight containers are a must.

Right after drying, package food in sealed bags (store supplies in single-meal or single-serving quantities to minimize repeated opening), and label the bags with the date. If you're drying in some quantity, store supplies in airtight barrels, large jars, or buckets. I like the 5-gallon (19 L) plastic buckets with snap-on lids (often available from cafeterias or restaurants). Then put the containers in a cool, dark place—a dry basement, closet, or pantry.

If you have the freezer space, you can really extend the shelf life of dehydrated supplies by freezing them until you leave for the backcountry. This is especially useful for foods with high fat content (such as meat or eggs).

From time to time, rummage through the bags to make sure none of the food has developed any mold. Once you head off on the trail, try to maintain the cool, dark, airtight conditions as much as possible.

CULINARY CONSIDERATIONS

It's the little things that elevate an outdoor menu from basic competence to elegance. Small touches add nuance to meals, fill the crannies in your companions' appetites, and enrich the food experience on a trip. None of them require a lot of extra effort, expense, or weight, so there's really no excuse not to include them in the food planning process.

VARIETY

Perhaps the most common failing of backcountry menus is sameness. Monotony earns serious demerits for camp cooks and menu-planners. Three days running of hot oatmeal for breakfast and crackers and cheese for lunch?—there's no excuse for such lack of vision and creativity. Variety is one of the easiest goals to accomplish in trip menu creation, and it will earn kudos on the trail.

Even if you have hot cereal three breakfasts in a row, make one grits, another oatmeal (see recipe page 35), and another cream of wheat (see recipe page 35). Instead of packing one big block of Cheddar, bring four small blocks of various cheeses. Make bannock (see recipe page 52) for lunch one day, have sandwiches the next (see recipe page 68), and then go to crackers (see recipe page 53). If you have dried eggs for breakfast several times, accompany one meal with hash browns and another with refried beans (see recipe page 40). Change the proportions in the trail mix, alternate rice, pasta, and grain entrées, then throw in bread and a stew for dinner one night. Purchase different varieties of hot soups.

See what I mean? Adding variety to the menu is more a matter of consciousness than anything. Just think varied, and you'll eat varied. Everyone will be happier, even on short trips that tempt you to succumb to that I-can-eat-anything-for-three-days mentality.

FRESH SUPPLIES

Doesn't food have to be vacuum-sealed, dehydrated, freeze-dried, or otherwise preserved to qualify as camp food? No. Sometimes, for example, on float trips without portages, you can carry a cooler, cook Cornish game hens for dinner, and enjoy eggs and bacon for breakfast. Even on backpacking trips or long trips, where weight concerns are a powerful motivation for drying everything in sight, you can handle a surprising amount of fresh foods.

Bulk cheeses will last for weeks, especially if the weather doesn't get too hot and you aren't squeamish about paring away the odd bit of mold. A couple of fresh onions will last up to a week and add great flavor to meals. Don't forget fresh garlic in your spice kit, either. Other hardy vegetables—cabbage, carrots, peppers, broccoli, and cauliflower—last for days or even longer, and add flavor and texture to a variety of dishes. Half a sautéed onion in an entrée, or a couple sliced peppers on a lunch bagel, can transform the meal.

SPICES AND CONDIMENTS

A complete spice or seasoning kit is important for creating variety. Fresh herbs from the garden are best, and dried herbs from a health food store are second best. Fill prescription bottles or film containers with an assortment of spices, and take with you their power to transform basic ingredients into a curry, an Italian sauce, or a sweet-and-sour dish. A carefully chosen spice kit weighs next to nothing but is the most powerful ingredient in the camp cook's arsenal.

Small and compact, condiments allow you to spice up trail fare. Hot sauce, tamari, hot mustard, and dried salsa are only a few of the myriad condiments available in grocery stores. Pack them with the spices to add punch to trailside meals.

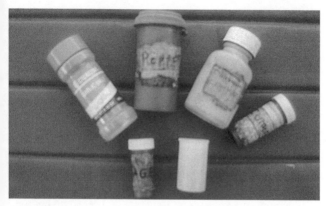

The toughest ammunition against breakfast boredom, lackluster lunches, and dinner drudgery is an adequate stock of spices and condiments. Gear up with power flavors such as Tabasco sauce, curry paste, wasabi, and horseradish. Just a wee bit goes a long way, so you can pack a huge culinary punch with very little space and weight.

APPETIZERS, DESSERTS, AND TREATS

Round out meals with before-and-after treats. If weight and bulk are a concern, you might not want to indulge on every dinner, but consider a ready-to-eat appetizer such as trail mix, energy bars, or nuts (see the Lunch and Snacks chapter), and a simple dessert, such as a fruit cup or Apple Heaven (see Hot Drinks and Desserts chapter). It's surprising how these extras can boost group morale and banish any lingering hunger pangs.

Once in a while, throw in a special treat for the day it rains from dawn to dark or the miles get particularly grueling. A handful of licorice, a jar of artichoke hearts, a small bottle of wine, or the 5-minute Blind Dates (see recipe page 129)— pretty soon the rain isn't as demoralizing as you thought.

EQUIPMENT

The style of your trip and your menus dictate how elaborate your kitchen set needs to be. A short backpack trip with a menu of simple, one-pot meals might require only a small pot. A car-camping or raft trip, for which weight wouldn't be a limiting factor, allows a more elaborate menu that might demand Dutch ovens, folding tables, and fire pans.

Much also depends on personal preference. Some people enjoy multicourse meals involving lengthy preparations. Others would just as soon concentrate on other aspects of the outdoors and keep meals simple and preparation minimal. Unless you plan to eat nothing but food that doesn't require cooking at camp, or depend solely on military-style rations that heat by themselves, you'll need cookware and utensils.

THE POT SET

Almost without exception, an outdoor trip will require at least one pot to prepare entrées and boil water for drinks. A two-quart pot is a good size for a group of two to four. A second pot just for hot water is also worth packing: while food is cooking in one pot, you can use the other to heat water for drinks or washing dishes. If the largest pot lid can't double as a fry pan, you may need a lidded frying pan for sautéing or frying. Nesting pot sets come in a variety of styles, are made from an amazing spectrum of materials, and sport a wide range of price tags. I tend to go fairly simply. Many pot sets come with gadgets and utensils you'll rarely need and that only add weight and clutter to your pack.

COOKING UTENSILS

In the minimalist camp, the only utensil you need is the cook's pot-stirring spoon, which doubles as the eating spoon. In most camps, however, a larger stirring spoon, a spatula, and pot-lifting pliers are needed. Review elaborate menus to ensure you bring any needed exotic camp utensils—shish kebab skewers, corn tongs, or marshmallow roasting forks.

EATING UTENSILS

Traditional mess kits assume we need the same dishware and cutlery at camp that we'd expect at home. In fact, the vast majority of camp meals can be consumed using only one cup, one bowl, and one spoon for each person. Your pocketknife will serve for the cutting and chopping jobs, and unless you'll be eating fresh meats, you probably won't need forks and knives. Start with cups, bowls, and spoons, and then add if you find it necessary.

BAKING DEVICES

Culinary vistas open up when you start baking in the backcountry. Suddenly you can enjoy breads, pies, quiche, pizza, and other delicacies that are otherwise unattainable in the woods.

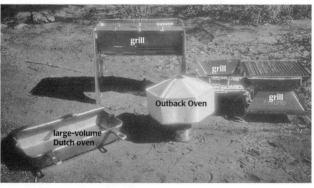

Outdoor baking and cooking devices are available in a broad range of designs so that anyone—car campers (using a rectangular Dutch oven designed for cooking in volume) to long-distance backpackers (using the very lightweight Outback Oven)—can enjoy fresh-baked treats in the wilderness. Several grills and reflector cooking designs allow campers to use wood or briquettes without making fire scars.

A traditional Dutch oven in action. Sandwiched between a thin layer of coals below and a generous layer on top, the oven will bake nearly anything you would bake in your home oven. It doesn't matter if you're a ravenous long-distance trekker or a car camper feasting on "three squares a day"—the aroma of freshly baked goodies is always a welcome treat at camp.

The **Dutch oven** is the traditional backcountry baker. This heavy pan is made from cast iron or cast aluminum—the latter is preferable because of its lighter weight. Either material is too heavy for backpacking or bike touring but serves well on river trips and car-camping jaunts. The Dutch oven is usually round, with a tight-fitting lid, and often stands on short legs that elevate the bottom above the heat source. In the field, pile a layer of coals (or charcoal briquettes) on top of the oven and a very thin layer underneath to bake goodies like Date Nut Bread (page 54), Sherherd's Pie (page 87), Shrimp Quiche (page 82), or Blueberry Cobbler (page 131).

Modern backpacking suppliers sell ovens for backpackers. The **Outback Oven** shown on the previous page is light enough to carry in a pack, and some backpacking ovens do double duty as both frying pans and ovens to be used on conventional camp stoves.

The **reflector oven** is made of collapsible, lightweight tin or aluminum panels that fold open to be set up next to an open fire. It works by concentrating the reflected heat for baking. This kind of oven has gone out of style, largely because open fires are often not an option. When a fire is the source of heat, however, a reflector oven is perfectly adequate for baking muffins while the soup pot simmers on the grill.

Even a **lidded frying pan** can function as a simple oven for baking goods such as flat breads and quesadillas, as long as the heat source can be turned down very low, or you place a layer of coals on the pan lid.

PRESSURE COOKERS

Small, lightweight pressure cookers specifically for camp cooking allow you to add dried beans, long-cooking grains, and meats to camp dishes without dragging out cooking times and using up precious fuel.

They are, however, bulky and cumbersome, and unless you're already accustomed to using a pressure cooker, you're not likely to get more than sporadic benefit from adding it to your camp kitchen. Instead, substitute faster-cooking ingredients—black-eyed peas instead of pinto beans, for example, or basmati instead of brown rice.

OTHER KITCHEN EQUIPMENT

Over time, you'll devise a preferred set of kitchen gear that you can adapt for different styles of backcountry travel. Here's the list I use.

- A lightweight, compact cutting board is handy, especially for fresh vegetables.

- A measuring cup can double as your drinking cup.

- A grill with short legs is an ideal surface for cooking over fires (see photo on page 26).

- A fire pan (flat, heat-resistant metal pan similar to a charcoal grill) contains and elevates a fire to prevent fire scars on the ground. Local regulations may require the use of fire pans in areas where fire scars are an environmental problem, regardless of whether wood is available or not.

- Reusable cloth coffee filter inserts, or combination thermos—press pots, are the best options for brewing coffee because they make the best brew with the least mess and garbage.

- A lightweight nylon kitchen tarp with corner grommets is a helpful protection against rain and hot sun. A 10-by-10-foot (3 by 3 m) tarp can shelter a group of four.

- A collapsible wash basin is handy for hauling water and cleaning up in the kitchen.

- A small, metal trowel is essential if you plan to bake with coals.

10 KITCHEN ESSENTIALS CHECKLIST

1. Nesting pot set (2 pots, frying pan, lids, pot-lifting pliers)
2. Mess kits (bowl, cup, cutlery), 1 for each person
3. Spatula (doubles as a stirring spoon)
4. Cutting board (doubles as a serving tray)
5. Matches or lighter
6. Camp stove, fuel, and windscreen, or grill with legs
7. Tarp
8. Collapsible wash basin
9. Sponge–scouring pad combo
10. Dish towel

STOVES OR FIRES

Camp etiquette has evolved away from cooking on open flames toward cooking on backcountry stoves. Both approaches have their pros and cons. Fires are problematic when they use up the dead wood in an area, produce scars (scorch marks on the ground), and coat cook pots with soot. In heavily used areas that have only small amounts of natural fuel available, stoves are more efficient and more environmentally responsible than open fires, but they're products of manufacturing processes that also impact the environment, they burn petrochemical fuels, and they produce waste in the form of empty canisters.

A fire evokes the ambiance of camping trips like nothing else, and it's still a viable and satisfactory option where dead and downed wood (driftwood along rivers and lakes, for example) is plentiful or where fire rings are already in place. You can mitigate the harmful environmental impact of fires by using a fire pan (see page 23) to prevent scarring the ground with scorch marks.

Camp stoves come in a daunting array of models, from heavy-duty multiburner stoves used on commercial raft trips, to tiny titanium canister-stoves that weigh under a pound. The available array includes stoves fueled by liquid fuels, canister rigs, or propane-butane blends. Some come with wind-screens, legs for stability, and a plethora of knobs, hookups, and accessories.

You can spend less than $20 and up to $1,000 on a stove depending on your needs and preferences. Determine what sort of camp

One of many models in a wide range of designs on the market, this small camp stove is ideal for short trips for which you're planning one-pot meals.

An environmentally conscientious camper built a "no-trace," minimum-impact fire on top of a mound of mineral soil. The soil mound is built on a tarp so that when the fire is out and the ashes cold, the soil can be returned to its source and covered so all trace of environmental disturbance is eliminated.

cook you are and what trips you tend to take, then do some shopping, read some magazine reviews, and search the catalogs for the option that suits you best. Consider not just the physical features and layout of the stoves, but the fuels each stove uses: it's often difficult to get white gas in foreign countries, for instance, and some canister fuels are more affordable and readily available than others. A few canister designs are recyclable or refillable, reducing the amount of waste the stove produces.

CONDITIONS THAT WARRANT THE USE OF FIRES

- Dead and downed wood is available in great quantity: driftwood-strewn riverbanks and little-traveled forests, for example, are appropriate firewood sources.

- Fire scars are not an issue: fire pans are used, fire grates are in place, or fires are built below tide line or high-water marks.

- Fire danger is low.

- Wood is small enough and dry enough to burn completely to ash.

WATER TREATMENT

Getting water that's safe to drink has become a major issue in the backcountry. The days of dipping a cup into a clear stream to slake your thirst are largely the stuff of memories and old-timers' stories. Few places remain where campers can still risk a drink straight from a water source, and in an era of global climate change and ubiquitous, insidious environmental threat, they are becoming even rarer.

The most common and well-known threat to water quality in the backcountry is *Giardia lamblia* (also known as *Giardia duodenalis*), but *Cryptosporidium* (also known as *Cryptosporidium parvum*), *Entamoeba histolytia*, and a variety of viral bugs have also joined the fray. Sedimentation, chemical pollution, and heavy metals can also compromise drinking water.

Bringing drinking water from home is the safest option (make sure the containers are also clean!), and a sensible one for boat and car trips. Two five-gallon (19 L) jugs will supply drinking water for two people for up to a week, depending on conditions, and you can use boiled local water for cooking and washing needs.

If you can't carry water from a safe source, boiling is the next most effective and thorough option. Bringing water to a boil kills most of the bad critters, but it won't destroy chemical compounds or some viral bugs. The old adage that you have to boil water for ten minutes is overkill: simply bringing the pot to a rolling boil does the trick.

Chemical treatment of water supplies with iodine or bleach destroys the majority of problematic bugs. Let water sit for half an hour after treatment, and mask any chemical taste by flavoring water with drink crystals. Allowing treated water to sit uncovered allows the chemical residues to dissipate naturally.

Many filtration systems use a variety of filter mediums to screen out the bad guys. Some systems are actually built into water bottles; others are bulky and expensive pumps. Research your options to determine which water treatments work best for your needs and budget.

Water safe to drink or cook with has become so rare in the back-country that filtering water drawn from any lake, river, or stream is now recommended. One of many filtration systems on the market, this one draws water from its source, filters out parasites and viral bugs, and pumps the purified water into a container for safe drinking or cooking.

PRETRIP FOOD PREPARATION

Creating a thorough menu, purchasing supplies, and then drying and packaging trip food is often the biggest logistical challenge of an outing. Best to start early, stay focused, share the work load, and distribute the chores among tripmates.

Well before a trip, discuss food preferences, favorite meals, allergies, and dislikes with the group members. Good ideas almost always come out of this process, and problematic areas are identified early on. Devise a menu based on that information, and solicit feedback to fine-tune meals before it's time to buy supplies.

Distribute food chores among trip mates so no one has to shoulder the whole job. For instance, if two couples are traveling together, each can plan and then, in the field, prepare half the dinners and breakfasts. Strategies like this tend to produce great meals on the trail because people want to show off their favorite and most elaborate recipes. If people outnumber the meals, delegate different people to plan and provide beverages, treats and desserts, or snacks and appetizers.

In the prep phase, minimize the amount of food packaging you take with you and thereby the resulting garbage you'll have to lug home. Be especially wary of cardboard boxes, glass jars, and copious packaging layers. Combine ingredients when possible (powdered milk with cereal, veggies that will cook together) to reduce the number of discrete packages and repackage supplies in double plastic bags or heavy, reclosable bags.

Organize your packing plan to avoid endless rummaging every time a meal rolls around. I pack food in color-coded stuff sacks for quick identification. Breakfasts in blue bags, for instance, lunch in red, and so on, so that in camp I know which bag to grab.

Making the time and effort during pretrip food preparation to organize and streamline provisions pays off enormously on the trail. You'll shoulder only what you need and want, minimize annoying pack clutter, find what you need without the frustration of rummaging for it, and pack out less garbage.

Some people methodically package and label each meal in a separate bag for use on a specific day on the trip. That's fine if you're that organized and detail-oriented. I like a certain amount of spontaneity, so I can match meals with weather conditions, the group's (or cook's) fatigue level, remaining daylight, and gastronomic whim.

Unless you're preparing for an extended expedition or dehydrating food in large quantities (see Dry Your Own, pages 13–16), storing food supplies is pretty simple. If you're like me, you have some stuff in the freezer, perishables in the fridge, and staples or dried food in plastic bags.

Before departure, I pack food organized by meal, in large plastic bags, and then put them in the right stuff sack (see previous page). That's it. With the exception of perishables you might have in a cooler, everything is separated by meal category and bagged in meal-sized quantity, ready for the trailside chef.

One last thing: bring along a spare bag, hipsack, or stuff sack for food you'll want to get at during the day. Every morning pack it with the day's snacks and lunch food so you reach into the same bag each time without having to sort through the trip's entire food stash.

If one person on the trip does the lion's share of food preparation and packing, thank them often and profusely, and remember that the only people with a right to complain about the meals are the ones who do the work.

Backcountry campers, especially, are never too young or too old to hear it again: *breakfast is the most important meal of the day*. Fuel yourself for peak performance and comfort through the active day ahead. An elaborate, relaxed morning meal or a quick, easy breakfast—either one can provide the nourishment you need, provided the planning and recipes are good.

STARTING IN ELEMENTARY SCHOOL, we are told that breakfast is the most important meal of the day. 'Course, many of us ignore that most mornings. But it's never truer than on wilderness trips. Breakfast fuels you through the miles, keeps you warm in bad weather, and allows you to operate at peak levels. If there's one meal to be faithful to on the trail, it's the one that starts each day.

These recipes include elaborate and simple fare, but all the dishes qualify as fuel that will last you until lunch. For quick starts, consider the hot and cold cereals. On more relaxed mornings, try the egg or potato recipes. Vary the morning fare with an occasional pancake recipe, or a fruit concoction prepared the night before.

Whatever you do, don't skip breakfast!

HOT AND COLD CEREALS

Marypat's Never-Miss Granola

1 c. dried fruit (apples, apricots, peaches are all good)
4 c. rolled oats
1 c. shredded coconut
1 c. chopped almonds
1 c. sunflower seeds
1 c. wheat germ
1/2 c. sesame seeds
1/2 c. honey
1/2 c. vegetable oil

Mix all but the last two ingredients in a large bowl. Heat honey and oil together in saucepan until just boiling, then pour over dried mixture and stir thoroughly. Spread on cookie sheets and bake in oven at 350°F for 20 minutes (or until browned and crisp), stirring frequently.

If you prefer soft rather than crisp fruit, add the dried fruit after baking instead of before.

Alan Kesselheim, *Trail Food*

Granola Athabasca

3 c. quick rolled oats
3/4 c. wheat germ
2 c. corn flakes or Wheat Chex
2 c. Grape Nuts cereal
1/2 c. sesame seeds
1 c. chopped pecans, almonds, or filberts
3/4 c. firmly packed brown sugar
2 t. cinnamon
2 t. vanilla
1/4 c. dried milk for each 1 c. cereal
1/4 c. dry coffee lightener for each 1 c. cereal

Combine the first 8 ingredients. Spread out in large, flat pans. Bake at 350°F for 15–20 minutes or until golden brown. Remove to a large bowl and sprinkle with vanilla. Stir well and cool completely. Store in air tight containers. Makes 12 cups.

To serve, add dried milk and dry coffee lightener to cereal and combine thoroughly. Add sliced fruit if desired. Sprinkle with dry cherry or strawberry Jell-O if desired. Moisten with either hot or cold water (adding *hot* water makes a delicious cereal) and stir.

Harriett Barker, *The One-Burner Gourmet*

Cinnamon-Orange Cream of Wheat

2 c. water
$1/3$ c. Cream of Wheat (original, not quick)
1 t. cinnamon
1 can (6 oz.) Mandarin orange segments, drained

Over a medium flame, bring water and, if desired, $1/4$ teaspoon salt to a boil. Add cereal, stirring to prevent lumping. Cook 7–10 minutes, taking care not to burn cereal. Just before serving, add cinnamon and oranges.

Don Jacobson, *The One Pan Gourmet*

Roman Oatmeal

$1/2$ c. quick-cooking oatmeal
$1/2$ c. instant Roman Meal cereal
$1/2$ t. salt
2 c. water
$1/4$ c. raisins
dried milk
1 T. molasses, corn syrup, or pancake syrup

Combine all ingredients in a saucepan. Bring to a boil and stir until mixture starts to thicken.

Cover and remove from heat. Let set 5 minutes.

Serve with reconstituted dried milk to which has been added molasses or syrup. Serves 2–3.

Harriett Barker, *The One-Burner Gourmet*

Granola Colorado

3 Shredded Wheat biscuits (original size), crushed
2 c. Grape Nuts cereal
1 c. All-Bran cereal
1 c. slivered almonds, broken
$1/2$ c. toasted coconut
$1/2$ c. brown sugar
$1/3$ c. wheat germ
16 small or 8 large dried figs, cut up and rolled in $1/2$ c.
   powdered sugar

Combine all ingredients and store in a tightly closed container. Makes 8 cups.

Harriett Barker, *The One-Burner Gourmet*

Oatmeal Plus

1 3/4 c. water
1 c. old-fashioned oats
1/2 c. walnut pieces
1/2 c. dried cranberries or raisins

Bring water to rolling boil. Add oats and cook until almost done, about 5 minutes. Add walnuts and fruit. Heat until oatmeal is completely cooked. Sprinkle with brown sugar if desired. Serves 2.

CAKES AND THEIR RELATIONS

Bunkers

3 c. flour
1 T. baking powder
$1/2$ t. salt
dash of sugar
$1/2$ t. nutmeg
enough milk or water to make a nonsticky dough

In a bowl, mix dry ingredients with a fork to combine. Add water or milk to make a dough.

Put small spoonfuls of dough into $1/2$ inch of hot bacon or sausage grease in a frying pan. Turn bunkers when bottoms are golden brown. (Cooking the first side with the pan covered helps make them light.) When golden on the other side, remove and drain. Serve hot with honey or jam, or plain alongside eggs, bacon, or sausage and hot drinks.

Garrett Conover and Alexandra Conover, *The Winter Wilderness Companion*

Crêpes (Very Thin Pancakes)

$1^1/2$ t. butter
$1/4$ t. salt
$1^1/2$ c. enriched flour
4 extra-large eggs
2 c. whole milk
$1/4$ c. olive oil

Combine butter, salt, and flour. Make a well in flour mixture and put in egg and milk (do not use water). With a fork, whip egg and milk together and gradually take up more and more flour until all is blended. Use a small amount of olive oil at a time to oil your skillet. Put $1/8$ cup batter into a hot, oiled skillet. Lift skillet from heat and rotate it until the batter is evenly spread over the bottom. Set skillet back on heat for 1 minute until batter is done. Separate the crêpe from the skillet carefully to avoid tearing. Follow the same directions until all batter is made into crêpes. Serve as desired. Makes 16 crêpes, which serve 4–6.

Jean and Samuel Spangenberg, *The Portable Baker*

Bacon-Cheese Oven Pancake

12 oz. biscuit mix
$3/4$ c. whole milk
1 extra-large egg
1 c. plus $1/2$ c. Swiss cheese, shredded
1 T. white granulated sugar
$1/4$ c. maple syrup
12 pieces bacon, cooked

Reserve maple syrup, bacon, and $1/2$ cup cheese for topping. Combine biscuit mix, milk (do not use water), and egg. Add remaining ingredients and mix well. Pour into a buttered skillet or pan. Top with cheese and bacon. Bake uncovered for 10−15 minutes at 375°F. Serve with maple syrup. Makes 4−6 servings.

Jean and Samuel Spangenberg, *The Portable Baker*

Pancakes

$1 1/2$ c. nonfat dried milk
$4 1/2$ c. flour
2 T. sugar
2 T. baking powder
1 t. salt
$1/2$ t. baking soda
$3/4$ c. powdered egg (see page 16)

Making your own dry pancake mix from scratch is cost effective, and taking premade mix to camp saves prep time at breakfast.

Combine all ingredients and store in an airtight container. Makes 6 cups dry mix.

To make pancakes at camp, simply add $1/2$ cup plus 2 tablespoons water and 1 tablespoon oil to 1 cup dry pancake mix to make 8 pancakes.

Kay Pastorius, *Cruising Cuisine*

Pancakes in a Sack

1 c. all-purpose flour
1 t. white or yellow cornmeal
1 t. brown sugar
3/4 t. salt
3/4 t. baking soda
1 t. baking powder
1 egg
1 c. milk

Mix the dry ingredients at home and place in bag. At campsite add the wet ingredients to the dry in a bowl and mix until blended but still lumpy. Preheat frying pan and rub a bit of vegetable oil into pan. Cook pancakes until golden brown; flip and cook other side. Serve with maple syrup and bacon or sausage.

Don Jacobson, *The One Pan Gourmet*

Granola Pancakes

1 c. granola
1/2 c. flour
2 t. baking powder
3/4 c. dried milk
2 T. melted margarine
1 1/2 c. water
1 egg

Combine the first 4 ingredients well. Stir in the remaining ingredients. Spoon batter on lightly greased frying pan or griddle. Brown both sides. Top with a fried or poached egg.

Harriett Barker, *The One-Burner Gourmet*

French Toast

2 or 3 eggs
2 or 3 slices bread, slightly stale (let stand in open air
    for half an hour)
1 t. vegetable oil

Preheat frying pan. In a bowl, beat eggs. Soak bread slices in egg mixture until thoroughly moist. Add oil to pan and place one or two slices bread in pan (depending on size of pan) to cook. Before flipping, allow to brown well. Remove to plate and serve with favorite topping—maple syrup, jelly, or powdered sugar.

Don Jacobson, *The One Pan Gourmet*

EGGS

Huevos Con . . .

    4 dried or powdered eggs (see page 16)
    seasonings to taste*
    1 c. cold water
    1 T. oil
    $1/5$ lb. (about 3 oz.) Cheddar or Swiss cheese, cubed

    Mix eggs and seasonings in cold water ($1/4$ cup per egg) and reconstitute for a few minutes. Don't be dismayed by the lumpy, watery appearance. Heat oil in skillet to medium temperature. Just before frying, add cheese to eggs. The eggs cook in a transforming flash: by the time the cheese melts, your huevos are huevoed. (Some cut-up lunch sausage is nice in the eggs, too, if you're a meat lover.) Serve with salsa if desired.
    * May be dried in advance with the eggs; dill and pepper are old standbys, but use whatever you prefer.
    On the Side. *Hash browns:* Simmer 1 c. dried potatoes in 1 c. water until moisture is absorbed. Salt and pepper to taste. Sauté in a little oil until brown. Push potatoes to side and pour in the eggs to cook.
    Frijoles: Pour hot water over 1 can (15 oz.) refried beans, dehydrated. Keep adding small amounts of water until the beans are the consistency you prefer, and let them soak at least 10 minutes. Fry in a little oil until heated throughout and slightly brown. Push beans to the side and pour in the eggs to cook.
    Bannock: Prepare bannock (see recipe page 52) the night before to shorten prep time. Slice the muffins in half and fry in a little butter before cooking the eggs. Pile the cheesy eggs on top of your buttery, toasted muffins.

Alan Kesselheim, *Trail Food*

Basic Omelette

2 or 3 eggs, at room temperature
1 T. water
pinch of black pepper
herb of choice (cilantro, tarragon, basil, dill weed)
2 t. unsalted butter
salt to taste
fillings (see below)

In a bowl, beat eggs with water until well combined. Add pepper and herb choice.

In an omelette pan, over high heat, melt butter until bubbly. Pour in eggs and stir with the flat side of a fork, shaking the pan with your other hand until eggs form a creamy mass. Top with filling ingredients and fold in half.

Salt to taste before serving (salt added during cooking tends to toughen the omelette). Makes 1 serving.

Fillings:

- cream cheese, smoked salmon, sliced onion
- avocado, mushrooms, green onion, tomato, and melted Monterey Jack cheese
- sautéed mushrooms, tomatoes, zucchini, and onions with melted Monterey Jack cheese
- sautéed potatoes, onions, bacon bits, and cheese
- spinach, mushrooms, and cheese

Kay Pastorius, *Cruising Cuisine*

Vegetable Eggs

1 T. vegetable oil
2 medium potatoes (3/4 c. or so), chopped
1/4 c. green pepper, chopped
1 small onion, chopped
salt and pepper to taste
2 eggs

Heat frying pan over medium heat. Add oil and sauté vegetables until browned, but not crisp. Add salt and pepper to taste. Break eggs over vegetable mixture and cover. Lower heat and cook until eggs are to your liking. Sprinkle with 1/4 cup of your favorite cheese and 1 tablespoon bread crumbs, if desired.

Don Jacobson, *The One Pan Gourmet*

Eggs Benedict

8 eggs
4 English muffins
8 thin slices broiled ham or Canadian bacon
1 recipe Jiffy Hollandaise sauce (see next recipe),
    or 1 pkg. dry instant Hollandaise sauce
1 t. paprika

Poach eggs. (If using a Dutch oven, fill half full with water and bring to a boil. Remove from heat. Add eggs to water and replace lid on Dutch oven for 3–5 minutes.)

Split and toast English muffins. Top each half with thin slice of broiled ham or Canadian bacon. Place a poached egg on the ham.

Prepare Hollandaise sauce and pour over all. Sprinkle with paprika and serve immediately. Makes 8 servings.

Sheila Mills, *The Outdoor Dutch Oven Cookbook*

Jiffy Hollandaise

$1/4$ c. sour cream
$1/4$ c. mayonnaise
$1/2$ t. mustard
1 t. lemon juice

Combine all ingredients. Cook and stir over low heat until heated through. Makes $1/2$ cup.

Sheila Mills, *The Outdoor Dutch Oven Cookbook*

Huevos and Tacos

2 or 3 flour tortillas
3 eggs
2 oz. Muenster cheese, chopped or shredded
dash of Tabasco or hot sauce
1 t. vegetable oil
1 avocado, diced
1 T. black olives, diced

Warm tortillas in dry frying pan; set aside in covered dish to keep warm. In a bowl, mix eggs, cheese, and hot sauce. Add oil to hot frying pan and scramble egg mixture. When done, remove from heat and stir in avocado and olives. Spoon onto warm tortillas, roll, and top with salsa (if desired).

Don Jacobson, *The One Pan Gourmet*

A.M. Sausage Burrito

1 T. peanut oil
2 flour tortillas
water
1/4 lb. ground sausage
2 eggs

Rub oil on one side of each tortilla. Roll loosely with oiled side out and place on steamer. Place steamer in pan, add 1/2 cup water to pan, and bring to boil. Heat tortillas about 1 minute. Remove pan from heat and remove cover.

Once steam clears, remove tortillas, unroll, and place half the sausage meat in each tortilla on unoiled side. Fold tortilla over meat to resemble a small pillow and return to steamer, seam down. Add water to make 1/2 cup and place steamer inside again.

Cover and bring to boil over medium heat. Cook 15 minutes after water boils.

For a solid beginning on breakfast, put two eggs alongside tortillas on steamer after water boils. To spice up the burrito, add diced green pepper and onion to meat before placing it in tortilla.

Don Jacobson, *The One Pan Gourmet*

Swiss Scrambled Eggs

2 T. margarine or bacon drippings
1 T. dried onion flakes
1/4 c. water
2 T. dried milk
1 t. Worcestershire sauce
1/2 c. cubed Swiss cheese
6 eggs, lightly beaten
salt and pepper to taste

Melt margarine or bacon fat; add dried onion flakes.

Combine water, dried milk, Worcestershire sauce, and cheese, and add to eggs.

Pour into frying pan and cook over low heat, stirring until set. Season with salt and pepper. Serves 3–4.

Don Jacobson, *The One Pan Gourmet*

McIntosh Surprise

2 medium apples
$1/3$ lb. sausage, fresh or precooked
2 eggs
salt and pepper to taste

Core apples from the top, but don't break through bottom. Using a spoon, hollow out each apple to make a little pocket, widening opening at top. Fill about two thirds with sausage. Place in oven pan. Break egg on top of sausage (sides of apple will hold egg in place). Bake in medium oven at least 30–35 minutes. Add salt and pepper to taste.

Don Jacobson, *The One Pan Gourmet*

Rice and Scrambled Eggs

$3/4$ c. salted water
$3/4$ c. instant rice
3 eggs
$1/4$ c. milk
$1/2$ t. Worcestershire sauce
1 t. dried onion flakes
$1/2$ c. shredded Monterey Jack cheese

Boil salted water. Add instant rice, stir, and let stand 5 minutes, covered, off the heat source.

Combine remaining ingredients. Add to rice and stir. Return to heat and cook until set. Serves 3.

Harriett Barker, *The One-Burner Gourmet*

Corned Beef Hash and Poached Eggs

2 cans (15 oz. ea.) corned beef hash
4 eggs
salt and pepper to taste

Heat hash in skillet or Dutch oven, stirring until broken up and mixed. Make four depressions in the hash with a spoon or spatula. Break a whole egg into each depression. Cover and simmer until eggs are poached, about 10 minutes. Sprinkle with salt and pepper and serve. Serves 4.

Cottage Cheese Omelette

4 eggs
$1/2$ c. milk
$1/2$ t. salt
dash of pepper
1 pkg. freeze-dried or dehydrated cottage cheese,
    rehydrated (or use fresh)
1 t. parsley flakes

Whisk eggs, milk, salt, and pepper together. Pour into greased skillet. When eggs begin to set, add cottage cheese and parsley flakes. Stir.

Cook until eggs are set to suit. Serves 2–3.

Harriett Barker, *The One-Burner Gourmet*

HEARTY GRAINS AND POTATOES

Expedition Hash

1 c. bulgur
1 dried onion
2$^1/_2$ c. water
black pepper to taste
garlic powder to taste
1 t. basil
1 T. cooking oil
1 T. soy sauce or tamari
$^1/_5$ lb. sharp Cheddar cheese

In saucepan, add water to bulgur and onion and bring to a boil. Toss in pepper, garlic powder, and basil and simmer until liquid is absorbed (15 minutes). Heat oil in skillet or pan and sauté bulgur mixture until it starts to brown. Right at the end, dribble on soy sauce or tamari and add cheese (I like it in chunks). When the Cheddar has melted into nice tasty globs, start eating.

Variations:

- use fresh instead of dried onion; sauté it slightly before adding bulgur mixture to the pan

- use dehydrated, grated cheese instead of fresh

- vary the seasonings: oregano, cilantro, or Cajun mix

- soak bulgur overnight and go immediately into the sauté phase

Alan Kesselheim, *Trail Food*

Road House Hash Browns

1 T. peanut oil
1 medium onion, chopped
1 large potato, sliced thin (unpeeled)
salt and pepper to taste

Heat frying pan over medium flame and add oil. Sauté onions in oil until tender, but not crisp. Add potatoes and seasonings—leftover bacon, salami, or other diced meat could also be added at this point, if desired—and continue cooking until potatoes begin to stick to pan. This goes well with meals that include red meats, but fits any meal. A real belly warmer.

Don Jacobson, *The One Pan Gourmet*

Fresh Potato Skillet

3–4 potatoes, in 1-inch cubes
2 T. olive oil
$1/2$ lb. pork sausage (optional)
$1/2$ onion, chopped
1 c. diced green pepper or broccoli
1 t. thyme
salt and pepper to taste
$1/4$ lb. sharp Cheddar cheese, cubed

Boil potatoes in saucepan until almost tender, 5–10 minutes. Drain and set aside. Heat olive oil in skillet or Dutch oven. Sauté sausage (if desired) and onion, then add potatoes at medium-high heat. Add vegetables and spices, stir occasionally while the potatoes brown. At end, add cubed cheese, stir in, and cover to melt. Serves 4.

FRUITS AND SYRUPS

Hot and Fruity Rice Pudding

1 qt. milk (1$1/3$ c. powdered in 1 qt. water)
$1/4$ c. each dried cranberries, cherries, and blueberries
   (or other fruit)
$3/4$ c. uncooked white basmati rice
$1/4$ c. (brimming) brown sugar
$1/2$ t. cinnamon
$1/2$ t. salt

Shake instant milk in a quart water bottle and pour into saucepan. As milk starts to heat on the stove, add fruit first and then everything else. Bring liquid just to a boil, stirring now and again, then cover and simmer very gently until all liquid is absorbed (20–30 minutes). Eat hot or cool.

Alan Kesselheim, *Trail Food*

Hot Peach Crumble

$1/4$ c. margarine, melted
$1/2$ c. brown sugar, firmly packed
$1/4$ c. chopped nuts
1 T. lemon juice
$1/2$ t. cinnamon
4 Shredded Wheat biscuits
1 can (17 oz.) sliced peaches, drained (reserve liquid)

Melt margarine in a frying pan and remove to bowl. Add brown sugar, nuts, lemon juice, and cinnamon and mix well.

Place biscuits in a single layer in frying pan and arrange peach slices on top. Spoon margarine mixture over the top. Heat, covered, until hot. Add peach juice reserved from can if too dry. Serves 2.

Harriett Barker, *The One-Burner Gourmet*

Dried Fruit Compote

1 c. dried fruit of choice (apples, peaches, pears, rhubarb . . .)
2 c. hot water
$1/2$ c. honey or loosely packed brown sugar
$1/2$ t. cinnamon
$1/2$ t. nutmeg (optional)
dried lemon or orange peel (optional)

Combine all ingredients and soak mixture in covered pan overnight. By morning the compote will be ready to gobble straight or to be added to your cereal bowl.

Alan Kesselheim, *Trail Food*

Sugar Syrup

1 pound dark brown sugar
1 c. water
dash of cinnamon (optional)

Variation:
$1/2$ c. white sugar
$1/2$ c. brown sugar
1 c. water

This is an appropriate maple syrup stand-in to use on pancakes and French toast. Combine ingredients and simmer until sugar is dissolved.

Harriett Barker, *The One-Burner Gourmet*

Making bread in the wilderness is a cinch and doesn't require a camp oven. Bannock biscuits—classic, quick camp bread—require only a frying pan, so even backpackers carrying minimal cook sets can enjoy fresh bread on the trail.

MANY OUTDOORSPEOPLE take trips that never include the bread end of the culinary spectrum. Too bad for them. These recipes broaden and enrich trip menus that might otherwise fall prey to the bland and repetitive doldrums. Many of them are less complicated than you'd expect, and some are best popped into the oven at home so they're ready to be served at camp. No-yeast breads or simple scones, for example, are quick and painless, but add a lot to a menu. There's nothing like sticky buns or raisin scones to take trip food to the next level of fresh excellence. (Don't miss the breads in the form of kuchens, cobblers, and crumbles at the end of the Hot Drinks and Desserts chapter!)

NO-YEAST BREADS, CRACKERS, AND BISCUITS

Basic Bannock

$1/2$ c. (brimming) white flour
$1/2$ c. (brimming) whole wheat flour
1 t. baking powder
$1/2$ t. salt
3 T. powdered milk
water

These are the timeless, tried-and-true ingredients for quick camp bread. We often cook biscuits in the evening to make a two-meal supply for two people. Mix dry ingredients thoroughly in a bowl (better yet, mix it and bag it at home) and add careful dribbles of water until dough is slightly sticky in your hands—*beware*: it's easy to overdo the water. Form into 4 scrupulously equal patties $1/2$ to 1 inch thick. Cook over medium heat in a lightly oiled skillet until browned on the outside and cooked through.

Variations:

- add different seasoning combinations, like garlic and chives, Cajun, cinnamon, or dill
- mix in dehydrated grated cheese, which will melt during cooking
- experiment with flours made from different grains
- add millet, oatmeal, wheat germ, or couscous
- mix in any number of ingredients for flavor, like raisins, onion, or sunflower seeds

Alan Kesselheim, *Trail Food*

Corn Bread

$13/4$ c. yellow cornmeal
$1/4$ c. whole wheat flour
$1/4$ c. powdered milk
3 T. baking powder
1 t. sea salt
1 egg, lightly beaten
1 T. honey
2 T. butter, melted (plus enough to grease Dutch oven)
$11/2$ c. milk

Butter a Dutch oven or 9-by-9-inch baking pan.

Combine cornmeal, flour, powdered milk, baking powder, and salt. Add egg, honey, butter, and milk, and stir until moist. Pour batter into Dutch oven or pan.

Bake in Dutch oven for 20 minutes, or in 425°F conventional oven for 20–25 minutes. Makes 6 servings.

Sheila Mills, *The Outdoor Dutch Oven Cookbook*

Angie's Cheese Crackers

1 c. unbleached all-purpose flour
1/4 t. baking soda
1/2 t. salt
1/2 c. cornmeal
1/4 c. wheat germ
1/2 c. butter (plus enough to grease Dutch oven)
2 oz. (1/2 c.) Cheddar cheese, grated
1/4 c. milk
1 T. vinegar

Liberally grease a Dutch oven or baking sheet and set aside.

Combine all ingredients to make dough. Roll out to about 1/4-inch thickness and pat into bottom of Dutch oven or onto baking sheet. Score lines in the dough with a fork for breaking the crackers.

Bake in Dutch oven for 15–20 minutes, or in 400°F conventional oven 15–20 minutes, until golden brown. Cool and break along scored lines. Yields 12 crackers.

Sheila Mills, *The Outdoor Dutch Oven Cookbook*

Big D's Biscuits

1/2 c. flour
1/2 t. baking powder
pinch salt (optional)
1 t. vegetable oil
1/4 c. water, approximate

Combine all ingredients, adding just enough water to make a good stiff dough. Flour your hands and make biscuits about 2 inches in diameter and 1 inch thick. Place on greased baking pan. Bake 10–15 minutes, checking to see that biscuits don't burn.

Don Jacobson, *The One Pan Gourmet*

Berry Bread

2 c. biscuit mix
2/3 c. milk
1 c. fresh berries, washed
1/2 c. sugar
margarine for cooking

Combine biscuit mix, milk, berries, and sugar. Spoon onto hot, greased frying pan and flatten with a spatula. Cook until brown on one side (about 5 minutes), turn, and brown the other side.
Makes 10–12 biscuits.

Harriett Barker, *The One-Burner Gourmet*

Date Nut Bread

2 c. boiling water
4 c. chopped dates
1 1/2 c. packed brown sugar
2 extra-large eggs (or powdered eggs, see recipe page 16, plus 1/2 c. water)
4 c. chopped English walnuts
4 c. enriched flour
1 t. salt
2 t. baking soda

Pour boiling water over dates, set aside. Combine sugar and eggs. Add remaining ingredients to egg mixture, including dates and any liquid from the dates. Bake in a greased loaf pan or Dutch oven 50–55 minutes at 350°F. Makes one loaf that serves 6–8.

Jean and Samuel Spangenberg, *The Portable Baker*

YEAST BREADS

Sinful Sticky Buns

Buns:
2 pkg. active dry yeast
$1/2$ c. warm water
2 c. warm milk
$1/2$ c. vegetable shortening
6 T. sugar
2 t. salt
2 eggs
6 $1/2$ c. unbleached all-purpose flour

Caramel Glaze:
1 c. (2 sticks) unsalted butter
3 c. brown sugar
$1/2$ c. light corn syrup
3 c. broken pecan or walnut pieces

Make buns: dissolve the yeast in the warm water. In a large bowl, mix milk, shortening, sugar, salt, and eggs until well blended. Add activated yeast and 4 cups of the flour; mix vigorously. Add the rest of the flour to make a soft dough. Knead for 1 minute. Let dough rest for 10 minutes, then knead again until dough is smooth and elastic. Cover and let rise until doubled in bulk.

Make caramel glaze: heat and stir butter, brown sugar, and corn syrup in a saucepan until butter is melted and sugar dissolved. Remove from heat and pour 1 cup glaze into a small bowl and set aside. Pour the remaining glaze over the bottom of a 12-inch Dutch oven or 9-by-12-inch baking pan and sprinkle nuts over the glaze.

Roll out dough into a rectangle and spread with the set-aside glaze. Roll dough up from the wide side into a long tube. Cut into 12 pieces, each about 1 $1/2$ inches long. Lay pieces flat side down atop nuts in the Dutch oven. Cover and let rise until puffy.

Bake in Dutch oven 25–30 minutes, or in 350°F conventional oven 30–35 minutes. Invert pan onto waxed paper. Serve warm. Makes 12 large buns.

Sheila Mills, *The Outdoor Dutch Oven Cookbook*

Cheesy Pepper Bread

1 pkg. ($1/4$ oz.) rapid-rise yeast
$1/8$ c. (2 T.) white granulated sugar
$1/4$ c. warm water
$21/3$ c. enriched flour
1 t. salt
$1/4$ t. baking soda
1 t. black pepper
1 c. cultured sour cream
1 extra-large egg
1 c. Cheddar cheese, shredded

Grease two 1-pound coffee cans. Combine yeast, sugar, and warm water. Set aside to activate. Combine remaining ingredients and gradually mix into yeast mixture. Knead dough several times, then divide in half. Put each half in a coffee can to rise for 30–40 minutes until double in bulk.

Bake at 350°F for 35–40 minutes. Cool before slicing. Makes two small loaves of 6 to 8 slices each.

Jean and Samuel Spangenberg, *The Portable Baker*

Jean's Pita Bread

1 pkg. ($1/4$ oz.) rapid-rise yeast
2 t. white granulated sugar
$11/2$ t. salt
1 c. water
2 T. olive oil (optional)
3 c. enriched flour
4 oz. sour cream powder (see page 106)

In a large bowl, combine yeast, sugar, salt, water, and oil. Gradually add flour and sour cream powder. Turn dough onto a floured surface and divide into four pieces. Flatten each piece and roll to about 6 inches in diameter and $1/8$ inch thick. Place pitas on an ungreased cookie sheet and let rest 10–15 minutes.

Bake 4–6 minutes in preheated 450°F oven until pitas puff up into balls. Remove pitas and let cool. To save space, you can flatten the pitas for storage. Makes 4 large pitas.

Jean and Samuel Spangenberg, *The Portable Baker*

SCONES

Baked Cinnamon Scones

butter for greasing Dutch oven
2 c. whole wheat flour
1 T. baking powder
1 T. sugar
$1/2$ t. salt
$1/2$ t. cinnamon
2 T. oil
$1/2$ c. buttermilk

Grease a Dutch oven or two baking sheets.

Combine dry ingredients in a large bowl. Stir in oil and buttermilk with a fork until mixture clings to itself. Knead dough gently for 3 minutes.

Divide dough into three parts. Roll out each part to $1/2$-inch thick. Cut into 6 wedges or use a small glass or cutter to cut into 2-inch rounds.

Bake in a Dutch oven 10–15 minutes, or in a 450°F conventional oven 10–15 minutes. Serve hot. Yields 18 scones.

Sheila Mills, *The Outdoor Dutch Oven Cookbook*

Raisin Scones

2 c. biscuit mix
$1/2$ c. raisins
2 T. sugar
$1/4$ t. orange drink crystals
$1/2$–$2/3$ c. milk, enough to make soft dough

Combine dry ingredients.

Stir in milk. When dough gathers into a ball, dust hands with flour and transfer dough to a floured cutting board. Shape dough into a 9-inch circle and cut with a sharp knife to make 12 triangles.

Cook 10 minutes on an *ungreased* heavy skillet over medium heat. Turn and cook 10 minutes longer. Makes 12 scones.

Harriett Barker, *The One-Burner Gourmet*

Some trips allow for a leisurely lunch break. In crisp weather a lunch that includes instant soup or hot chocolate will let you linger comfortably to enjoy an outlook or a little reading.

LUNCH IS THE MOST DIFFICULT trail menu to vary: it's tough to come up with different sandwich, fruit, and nut combinations that work well in the backcountry. More than in any other meal category, when planning lunch menus, put some effort into adding condiments, varying cracker and cheese options, thinking about different spreads, and alternating fruit and trail mix. A little variety in the middle of the day will go a long way toward ensuring trip satisfaction. A good selection of snacks is also critical in keeping morale up and bridging the gap between meals when conditions are demanding.

SPREADS

Magic Mediterranean Hummus

1 1/2 c. raw garbanzo beans (chickpeas), soaked overnight,
    cooked until soft (1–2 hours), and drained
3 cloves fresh minced garlic
1 1/2 t. salt
pinch cayenne
dash of tamari
juice from 2 lemons
3/4 c. tahini
1/2 c. minced parsley
1/2 onion, finely chopped

Hummus is a piquant antidote to the peanut butter blues. It makes a great spread for crackers or bannock. If you have a food processor, throw everything in and zing it into a homogenous paste. If not, mash garbanzos first, then mix in the other ingredients. Spread thinly onto solid dehydrator trays and dry at 130°F until crumbly. Powder the dried mix in a blender. In the field, reconstitute with warm water, but be careful to add water slowly: a little too much leaves you with hummus soup. Makes enough spread for three lunches for two people.

Variations:

- some people like more—or less—garlic, tamari, or tahini
- try other beans, such as black or Anasazi beans

Alan Kesselheim, *Trail Food*

Peanut and Jelly Spread

1/2 c. peanuts
1 1/2 T. soft margarine
1/2 c. orange marmalade

Chop peanuts in a blender. Combine all ingredients and mix well.

Harriett Barker, *The One-Burner Gourmet*

Ann and Phil's Lentil Pâté

1 c. lentils
3–4 c. water
2 c. stir-fried vegetables (carrots, peppers, onions,
    and mushrooms)
2 cloves fresh garlic, minced
1 t. basil
1 t. dill
1/2 c. cashews or sunflower seeds

Another nice lunch spread for bannock or crackers that will keep you out of the clutches of peanut butter overdose. Cook lentils until tender. Meanwhile, stir-fry veggies with spices, then add them to lentils and continue cooking until everything is very tender. Add nuts or seeds and purée everything in a blender. Dry on trays at 135°F until all the moisture is gone (8–14 hours). Crumble the dried mix or powder it in the blender. Bring it back to the desired consistency on the trail with warm water. Remember, be careful not to add one slurp of water too many!

Alan Kesselheim, *Trail Food*

Herbed Cheese Spread

8 oz. yogurt cheese or cream cheese
1 clove garlic, finely chopped
1 T. dried parsley or 2 T. fresh
1/2 t. dried thyme
1 t. freshly ground black pepper

Combine cheese with spices and stir well. Store in the refrigerator. The spread keeps for about two weeks. Makes 1/2 cup.
Other uses for yogurt cheese:

- for a dip to be served with fresh veggies, combine 1 ounce Hidden Valley Ranch Dry Dressing Mix with 2/3 cup yogurt cheese and 1/3 cup mayonnaise

- for a seafood spread with crackers, combine yogurt cheese with chopped olives and minced clams

Kay Pastorius, *Cruising Cuisine*

ENERGY BARS AND LOGS

Pemmican

2 c. animal fat
1 c. bacon drippings
2 c. finely ground dried meat (jerky)

Melt together fat and drippings. Pour over jerky. Sprinkle with salt, pepper. Let harden in tuna cans with lids removed. Loosen pemmican by dipping cans partway into hot water. Remove pemmican and wrap in waxed paper. Recipe fills 4 tuna cans (12 oz. ea.).

Dried berries (2 cups) can be added for carbohydrate content and extra flavoring. However, a true pemmican contains only fat and meat.

Garrett Conover and Alexandra Conover, *The Winter Wilderness Companion*

Trail Bars

$1/2$ lb. pitted dates
1 c. peeled, cored and sliced apples (or use dry ones)
1 c. seedless raisins
2 c. crushed vanilla cookies
$1 1/2$ c. chopped nuts
1 c. powdered sugar
1 c. granulated sugar
$3/4$ c. honey
$1/2$ t. vanilla
water, if needed

Put first three ingredients through fine blade of food grinder. Combine cookies, nuts, and both sugars, and add to fruit. Add honey, vanilla, and water.

Knead and work with hands to mix well. Press into foil-lined pan. Allow to "dry" for a few hours. Remove from pan by lifting the edges of the foil. Cut into bars and roll in brown sugar. Wrap bars individually in foil or plastic wrap. Store in refrigerator.

Harriett Barker, *The One-Burner Gourmet*

Winter Expedition Fruitcakes

2 sticks (1/2 lb.) butter
1 c. honey
2 T. lemon juice
3 eggs
2 c. chopped cranberries
3 c. flour
3 t. baking powder
1 t. salt
1 c. dried milk
3 t. ground ginger (or 2 T. candied ginger)
2 t. each nutmeg, cardamom, and rosehip flour
2 c. chopped dates
2 c. chopped nuts
2 c. chopped apricots
3 c. muscat raisins, currants, or both

These fruitcakes can be made well in advance if stored in a cool, dry place.

Melt butter and add honey. Blend lemon juice, eggs, and washed, sorted cranberries in a blender (or chop the cranberries coarsely and mix them with the juice and the eggs). Blend briefly and add the butter-and-honey mixture. Now add these wet ingredients to the remaining ingredients. Pour into 3 greased 1-pound coffee cans until 3/4 inch from top. Bake at 325°F until a knife inserted in the middle comes out clean. Makes 3 fruitcakes.

Garrett Conover and Alexandra Conover, *The Winter Wilderness Companion*

Quick Energy Logs

1/4 c. dry-roasted cashews (unsalted)
1 c. walnuts
1/2 c. figs
1/2 c. pitted dates
1/2 c. raisins
1/4 c. chopped dry apples
1/2 t. lemon juice
1/2 c. flaked coconut

Put nuts and fruits through food grinder two times. Add lemon juice and mix. Roll into small logs. Roll logs in coconut and let stand several hours to dry.

Wrap individually in foil and store in refrigerator until ready to use.

Harriett Barker, *The One-Burner Gourmet*

Date Wheat Bars

1 1/2 c. packed brown sugar

3 eggs, beaten well

1/4 t. salt

1/2 t. vanilla

1 c. whole wheat flour

1 c. chopped nuts

1/2 c. chopped dates

This recipe is easy and quick to make at home. Combine sugar and eggs. Add remaining ingredients, mix thoroughly, and pour into 2 greased 7-by-11-inch pans.

Bake at 325°F about 25 minutes. Makes 40 bars.

Harriett Barker, *The One-Burner Gourmet*

Fruit Energy Bars

1 c. vegetable oil

1 c. packed brown sugar

1 fresh egg

1 c. milk

2 T. vanilla

2 t. cinnamon

1 t. nutmeg

1/2 t. powdered ginger

2 c. flour (whole wheat and white blend)

1 t. baking soda

2 c. dried fruit pieces (apricots-apples-peaches blend is a winner)

1 c. chopped walnuts

3 c. rolled oats

1 c. wheat germ

chocolate chips (optional)

Mix together each group of ingredients. In order, add groups to first group, mixing after adding each group. Spoon dough evenly onto greased baking sheet or shallow pan (12 by 18 inches). Bake at 350°F until browned (20–30 minutes). When cool, cut into trail bars.

Alan Kesselheim, *Trail Food*

LEATHERS, NUTS, AND ASSORTED SNACKS

Fruit Leather Trail Snack

2 c. puréed fruit
water or fruit juice as needed

Almost any fruit can be made into leather, but juicy varieties like oranges have too much pulp and liquid to be convenient. Apricot, apple, peach, plum, and pear all make good leathers. Fresh fruit is superior, but frozen or canned is also feasible (pour off liquid or syrup).

Cook fruit (if necessary) until soft but not pulpy, and purée in blender or food processor until quite smooth (add a touch of extra water or fruit juice if needed).

Pour liquid evenly onto solid dehydrator trays and dry at 130°F until leathery and free of moisture pockets. Peel leather sheets off trays and roll up (roll on a sheet of plastic wrap to avoid sticking). Cut into handy lengths for packing or snacking, and wrap or bag in plastic. Eat on the trail as is, or reconstitute in warm water (half as much water as fruit) to make fruit sauce (great baby food!).

Variations:

- make combination leathers, such as apple-banana, apricot-pineapple, pear-rhubarb, peach-strawberry

- add a slight amount of honey or brown sugar for a sweeter taste

- flavor with cinnamon, allspice, lemon peel, or ginger

- garnish with coconut, granola, chopped nuts, or other treat before drying

Alan Kesselheim, *Trail Food*

Miss Sue's Herky Jerky

8 lb. raw, lean meat (beef round or chuck, or venison)
1 T. salt
1 1/2 T. garlic powder
1 t. black pepper
1 T. ginger
2/3 c. brown sugar
1 c. teriyaki sauce
1 c. soy sauce or tamari

Slice meat in thin strips, cutting across the grain (slightly frozen meat is easier to cut). Combine meat with remaining ingredients in a large bowl, and marinate in the refrigerator at least overnight (a plastic bowl with a tightly fitting snap-on lid is convenient because you can shake it to coat the meat evenly). Dehydrate at 140°F until pieces break when you bend them. Eat as is, or cook in eggs, stews, and chilis, but ration yourself, or it'll disappear before you know it. Makes roughly 2 pounds jerky.

Alan Kesselheim, *Trail Food*

Lemony Jerky 1

2 T. fresh lemon juice
1/4 c. olive oil
1 t. salt
1/4 t. black pepper
1 lb. meat, sliced

Mix all ingredients except meat. Add meat, cover, and refrigerate 2–4 hours before drying (see instructions in Miss Sue's Herky Jerky, above).

Alan Kesselheim, *Trail Food*

Lemony Jerky 2

1 c. pineapple juice
2 t. soy sauce or tamari
2 t. fresh lemon juice
2 cloves fresh garlic, minced
1 lb. meat, sliced

Mix all ingredients except meat. Add meat, cover, and refrigerate 2–4 hours before drying (see instructions in Miss Sue's Herky Jerky, above).

Alan Kesselheim, *Trail Food*

Other Jerkies I Have Known

Beef and game are standard jerky fare, but don't stop there. Here are some other options.

- Lamb: use leg or shoulder cuts.
- Ham: cooked and sliced (raw pork is taboo!).
- Fish: whitefish is good dried, especially if first marinated in a lemon or soy sauce. In general, less-oily fish dry best. Clean fish and fillet into thin strips before drying at 140°F.
- Tofu (blocks of soy bean curd): cut in 1/4-inch strips, marinate for an hour or two, and dry at 130°F until just slightly pliable.
- Turkey, cooked and sliced: marinate if you like, then dry until not quite brittle.

Alan Kesselheim, *Trail Food*

Zesty Zucchini Chips

firm, fresh zucchini in 1/4- to 3/8-inch slices
garlic salt to taste

Wash zucchini. Slice, spread onto trays, and sprinkle with garlic salt. Dry at 130°F until brittle. Take an extra bag of these chips, because the first one will be gone before you get to the trailhead.
Flavor variations:

- sprinkle with Cajun spices
- dip in tamari, barbecue sauce, or mustard sauce
- sprinkle with dill
- sprinkle with salt and vinegar

Alan Kesselheim, *Trail Food*

Salted Soybeans

Wash and soak raw soybeans in warm water overnight. Drain and place on paper towels to dry. (To speed drying, spread on rimmed cookie sheet and bake in a slow oven a few minutes.)

Deep-fry in hot oil for 10 minutes or until golden brown. Drain on paper towels and sprinkle with salt. Store in an airtight container.

Harriett Barker, *The One-Burner Gourmet*

Grilled Cream Cheese and Olive Sandwiches

8 slices whole wheat bread
4 T. butter
8 oz. cream cheese, softened
1 can (10¹/₂ oz.) pitted black olives, sliced

Butter both sides of all bread slices. Spread cream cheese generously on four slices and sprinkle olive slices over cream cheese. Top each with remaining slices of bread.

Grill in skillet, on Dutch oven lid, or in bottom of Dutch oven until bread is golden brown and cheese is soft. Cut sandwiches in half and serve. Makes 4 servings.

Sheila Mills, *The Outdoor Dutch Oven Cookbook*

Toasted Pumpkin or Sunflower Seeds

2 c. shelled pumpkin or sunflower seeds (available in health food stores)
2 T. Worcestershire or soy sauce
2 T. melted margarine
2 T. grated Parmesan or Romano cheese
salt, regular or garlic, to taste

Mix all ingredients in a bowl. Spread in a flat, oblong pan. Toast in 375°F oven, stirring every 5 minutes for 15 minutes or until browned.

Toasted seeds are delicious sprinkled on crackers or bread that's been spread with peanut butter, soft cheese, honey, or any sticky topping. Press cracker or bread upside down on the toasted seeds. These seeds are also delicious on ripe bananas, apples, mixed with scrambled eggs, or cooked in macaroni and cheese, to name but a few uses.

Harriett Barker, *The One-Burner Gourmet*

Dry Cereal Snack

6 c. Miniature Shredded Wheat
6 c. Rice Chex
6 c. Corn Chex
1 jar dry-roasted mixed nuts
1 envelope onion soup mix
6 T. melted margarine

In a large bowl, combine all ingredients except margarine. Add margarine and mix thoroughly.

Spread in a shallow pan. Bake at 300°F for 10 minutes, stirring at least once. Store in an airtight container.

Harriett Barker, *The One-Burner Gourmet*

One-Burner Fondue

2 c. plain croutons
3/4 lb. sharp Cheddar cheese, shredded
1 small can evaporated milk, plus water to make 3/4 cup
1 t. dry mustard
1/4 t. salt
dash of pepper
1 egg, slightly beaten
1 T. margarine
French bread, sliced

Stir croutons, cheese, milk, and seasonings in top of a double boiler.

Place over hot water. Stir constantly until cheese melts and the mixture thickens.

Whip egg and add with margarine to cheese mixture. Cook, stirring, about 5 minutes.

Scoop up mixture with French bread. Serves 3–4.

Harriett Barker, *The One-Burner Gourmet*

Soup or stew, with bannock to wipe the bottom of the bowl, is hearty comfort food for chilly weather. Soup is one of the ultimate easy one-pot meals. And fun—soups and stews offer camp cooks limitless flexibility, experimental leeway, and creative license for concocting with whatever they like from what's on hand.

BACKCOUNTRY TRAVELERS often neglect soup and stew possibilities when planning menus. Fact is, they are great options for cold-weather entrées, can complement other dinner entrées, provide a complete dinner on a less rigorous day, or make a hot lunch for a day spent in camp. Served with a batch of bannock or yeast muffins, soups and stews are a hearty meal option and a welcome variation in camp fare.

SOUPS AND CHOWDERS

Barley-Mushroom Medley

6–7 c. water
1 cube vegetable bouillon
1/2 c. raw barley
1/2 c. dried mushrooms
1–2 dried onions
2 T. tamari or soy sauce
1 t. salt
1 t. dill
pinch of pepper
2 cloves fresh garlic, minced
generous spoonful butter or margarine

This soup takes an hour or so to make, but your investment of time and fuel will reward you with a hearty dinner entrée. Bring water, bouillon, barley, and dried veggies to boil. Simmer about 30 minutes, until barley starts to plump up. Add tamari and seasonings and continue simmering until barley is tender, adding water as necessary. Spoon in butter for the last little bit of cooking time. (Using cooked and dried barley hastens this soup to your bowl.)

Alan Kesselheim, *Trail Food*

Potato-Onion Soup

6 c. water
1 vegetable or chicken bouillon cube
1 1/2 c. dried potatoes
1/4 c. dried celery
1/4 c. dried carrots
salt and pepper to taste
1 t. basil
1 T. butter or margarine
2/3 c. dried milk powder
1 fresh onion, chopped

The fresh onion makes this recipe, although dried onion works, too. Boil dried veggies and bouillon in water 15–20 minutes, or until veggies are nearly tender. Add remaining ingredients. Continue simmering over very low heat until onion is tender and all is an evocative, savory blend.

Alan Kesselheim, *Trail Food*

Corn Chowder

4 c. water
1 dried onion
$1/4$ c. dried celery
1 dried green pepper
1 c. dried corn
salt to taste
plenty of black pepper
large pinches of thyme and dill
$1/2$ t. basil
1 chicken or vegetable bouillon cube
2 T. butter or margarine
$1/3$ c. dried milk powder

Combine dried veggies and water in pot and bring to a boil. Reduce heat and simmer 5 minutes, then add seasonings and bouillon. Continue simmering until veggies are tender; add water if necessary.

Finally, dollop on the butter and powdered milk, then turn heat way down so the chowder barely bubbles, stirring to blend.

Variations:

- toasted bannock goes along nicely (see recipe page 52)

- if you can tote the extra weight, replace the dried milk with a can of evaporated milk for an extra-rich texture

Alan Kesselheim, *Trail Food*

Toni's Garlic Soup

4 c. water
1 large head (14–16 cloves) garlic, cloves smashed and peeled
$1/3$ c. olive oil
1 can ($14^1/2$ oz.) crushed Italian plum tomatoes
1 T. ground black pepper
1 c. small pasta, such as acini di pepe (seed shaped), orzo
    (rice-shaped), or angel hair (broken in small pieces)

Bring the water to a boil and add garlic and olive oil. Bring back to a boil and add tomatoes and black pepper. Boil soup vigorously for about 15 minutes, until it has slightly reduced in volume and begins to thicken. Add pasta and cook until tender. Serve immediately. Makes 4 servings.

Kay Pastorius, *Cruising Cuisine*

Soups and Stews

Fast Pea Soup

2 1/2 c. water
1/4 t. salt (optional)
1 c. freeze-dried or dehydrated peas (more for thicker soup)
1/2 c. ham, diced
1 carrot, diced
1/2 t. thyme

In pot over medium flame, bring salted water to a boil. Add all ingredients and cover. Simmer 45 minutes or longer to cook down peas, stirring occasionally. Serve with soda crackers or bread.

Don Jacobson, *The One Pan Gourmet*

STEWS

Trail Chili

6–8 c. water
1 c. dried black-eyed peas
1 c. dried veggie mix (see recipe page 117)
1 can (4 oz.) dried green chilis
$1/2$ c. sun-dried or dehydrated tomatoes
1 dried onion
1 t. cumin
1 t. basil
1 clove fresh garlic (or powder to taste)
1 t. salt
1 T. chili powder (or to taste)
pinch of cayenne
3 T. dried tomato sauce

Cook peas and dried veggies in boiling water 20 minutes, or until peas start to soften. Stir in remaining ingredients and cook until peas are tender, adding more water if necessary. Adjust seasoning to taste.

Variations:

- sprinkle with grated Parmesan or Monterey Jack cheese

- add dried, cubed tofu, dried hamburger, stew meat, or crumbled jerky to cook with veggies

- garnish with sour cream from an envelope mix (see page 106)

Alan Kesselheim, *Trail Food*

Big-Time Beef Stew

1 c. flour
$1/2$ lb. stew beef, cut in 1-inch cubes
2–3 T. vegetable oil
2 c. water
2 medium potatoes, unpeeled, scrubbed, and cubed
1 medium onion, cut in chunks
2 carrots, cut in chunks
salt and pepper to taste
1 bay leaf
1 t. Worcestershire sauce
celery seed to taste
1 egg, beaten

Place flour in bowl and dredge meat in flour. Over medium flame, heat pot and add oil. Brown floured meat, turning to prevent sticking. Save leftover flour. Add water to pot and scrape with spoon. Add all other ingredients, cover, and simmer at least 30 minutes. Stir occasionally.

Mix leftover flour with a little water, a few dashes of vegetable oil, and the beaten egg to make a sticky dough. With oiled spoon, drop balls of dumpling dough into stew, cover pan again, and cook 5 more minutes. *Do not stir* stew after adding the dumplings.

Don Jacobson, *The One Pan Gourmet*

Easy Lentil Stew

6 c. water
1 c. lentils
1 c. dried veggie mix (see recipe page 117)
1 dried onion
1 beef bouillon cube
garlic and pepper to taste
soy sauce or tamari to taste
$1/5$ lb. (about 3 oz.) sharp Cheddar, cubed

Bring water, lentils, and veggies to a boil. Simmer for 30 minutes, until lentils are tender. Add more water if necessary. While the pot bubbles, stir in all remaining ingredients except cheese. Just before serving, add cheese and stir until it melts completely (or place cheese in individual soup bowls so the pot is easier to clean).

Alan Kesselheim, *Trail Food*

Campfire Stew

2 lb. ground beef
1 onion, peeled and diced
2 cans condensed vegetable soup
salt and pepper

Try this awesome meal the first day of hiking so the hamburger doesn't go bad. Add salt and pepper to the hamburger and mix thoroughly. Roll pieces of hamburger into small balls.

Cook the hamburger with the onion in a large pot over the campfire or on a camp stove. Cook until the onion is translucent and the hamburger is well browned. If necessary, pour off the excess fat, dig a "cat hole" well away from camp, and carefully bury the fat.

Add the vegetable soup and enough water to keep it from sticking. Cover and cook slowly at least 20 minutes to cook the meat through. Serve hot. Serves 6–8.

Victoria Logue, Frank Logue, and Mark Carroll, *Kids Outdoors*

Souper Cluck Stew

$2^1/_2$ c. water
1 chicken breast half, cooked and cut in chunks
3 chicken bouillon cubes
2 potatoes, peeled and diced
1 carrot, chopped
1 medium onion, chopped
$1/_4$ t. cayenne pepper
1 clove garlic, crushed
$1/_4$ t. pepper
$1/_2$ c. dried corn
1 small tomato, quartered
flour (optional)

Place all ingredients except corn and tomato in pot over medium to high flame. Bring to boil, cover, and reduce heat. Simmer 30 minutes. Add corn and tomato and continue to simmer another 15 minutes. Add more water as needed. Thicken with flour if needed.

Don Jacobson, *The One Pan Gourmet*

Carrot and Lentil Stew

$1/2$ c. lentils
1 large carrot, diced
1 medium onion, diced
1 garlic clove, crushed
1 large tomato
4 c. cold water
1 t. parsley
1 bay leaf
black pepper to taste
chili powder to taste (optional)
pinch of salt

Add all ingredients except salt to cold water in pot (increase amount of water if you prefer a soupy stew). Bring to a boil and simmer 45 minutes or until lentils are soft. Add salt last (adding it before slows down cooking), and adjust seasonings. Cooking time can be shortened if lentils are soaked beforehand in hot water. Serve with whole-grain bread.

Don Jacobson, *The One Pan Gourmet*

Red-Eye Stew

1 T. margarine
$1/2$ lb. stew beef, cut in small cubes
1 medium onion, chopped
$1/2$ t. salt (optional)
1 t. paprika
$1/4$ t. caraway seeds
1 can (6 oz.) tomato paste
1 beef bouillon cube dissolved in 1 c. hot water
2 medium potatoes, cubed

In baking pan, melt margarine over medium flame and brown beef. Reduce heat and sauté onions. Remove from heat and add all ingredients except potatoes. Cover and bake 1 hour in medium oven. Add potatoes and cook another 30 minutes. Serve with hard rolls.

Don Jacobson, *The One Pan Gourmet*

Zucchini Stew

1 lb. ground beef
1 egg
4 T. dry bread crumbs
$1/4$ t. salt
dash of pepper
1 can mushroom gravy
1 lb. zucchini, cut in 2-inch slices
$1/2$ t. basil
1 large tomato, cut into chunks

Combine meat, egg, bread crumbs, salt, and pepper. Shape into small balls. Brown meatballs in a skillet. Drain fat and add gravy, zucchini, basil. Cook over a low flame 15–20 minutes. Add tomato and simmer 5 minutes longer. Serves 2–3.

Harriett Barker, *The One-Burner Gourmet*

It doesn't take long for a diet of trail mix and energy bars to lose its charm and for your stomach to start calling out for stick-to-your ribs, hearty cuisine. A Dutch oven allows you to prepare at camp just about anything you'd cook in your home oven. One-pot casseroles, pies, quiches, baked chicken and potatoes, BBQ ribs, pizza, enchiladas, shepherd's pie. . . . These and similar hearty entrées will send mouth-watering aromas drifting through camp, draw heartfelt ooohs and aaahs from trip mates, and satisfy the stomach grumbles.

BAKING DINNER ENTRÉES in the outdoors is an art worth practicing. No other cooking method melds flavors, melts cheese, and brings a dish to a bubbling crescendo quite like baking does—and it doesn't always require a bed of fire coals, either. When open fires aren't an option, try using charcoal briquettes, or lightweight Outback Ovens, which are specifically designed for use on camp stoves—see page 22. All Dutch oven recipes can also be prepared in Outback Ovens using the same directions. Some recipes include oven temperature settings, which are helpful if you bake dishes at home before a trip. In the field, they serve as general temperature guidelines. Once you experience freshly baked entrées, camp cooking will never be the same again.

Dutch Oven and Outback Oven Dinners

FISH

Shrimp Quiche

pastry for 10-inch single-crust pie
1 can (5 1/2 oz.) whole shrimp, well drained
1/3 c. chopped scallions (tops included)
4 oz. (1 c.) Swiss cheese, grated
3 eggs
1 c. milk
1/2 t. salt
1/8 t. pepper

Prepare the Pastry Crust for Double-Crust Pie recipe below, halving the ingredients for a single crust, or use a pie crust mix.

Line the bottom of Dutch oven or 9-inch pie dish with pastry dough. Distribute shrimp over the bottom of pastry. Sprinkle evenly with the scallions and cheese.

In a bowl, beat together eggs, milk, salt, and pepper. Pour over shrimp and cheese.

Bake in Dutch oven 35–40 minutes, or in 350°F oven about 45 minutes, or until custard is firm in the center. Let stand 10 minutes before serving. Makes 6–8 servings.

Sheila Mills, *The Outdoor Dutch Oven Cookbook*

Pastry Crust for Double-Crust Pie

2 c. unbleached all-purpose flour
1 t. salt
2/3 c. shortening
5–7 T. cold water

Mix flour and salt. Cut in shortening with pastry blender or fork until pieces are the size of small peas. Sprinkle water over mixture. Gently toss with a fork until moist.

Divide dough for top and bottom crusts and form into two balls. Flatten on lightly floured surface. Roll from center out to 1/8-inch thickness.

Fold dough into quarters and lift into Dutch oven or pie plate. Shape edges as desired. Proceed with recipe instructions.

(For single-crust pies requiring a prebaked crust, bake in Dutch oven 10–12 minutes, or in 450°F conventional oven 10–12 minutes.)

This recipe makes enough dough for an 8-, 9-, or 10-inch double-crust pie. For recipes requiring a single-crust pastry shell, halve the ingredients.

Sheila Mills, *The Outdoor Dutch Oven Cookbook*

Salmon Cheese Casserole

1 can (16 oz.) salmon, with liquid
4 oz. fresh mushrooms, or 1 can (4 oz.) mushrooms,
    drained and sliced
1$1/2$ c. bread crumbs
2 eggs, beaten
4 oz. (1 c.) Cheddar cheese, grated
1 T. lemon juice
1 T. minced onion

Flake fish in a bowl, removing all bones. Add all remaining ingredients and mix thoroughly. Pour into Dutch oven or 1$1/2$-quart casserole dish.

Bake in Dutch oven 30–35 minutes, or in 350°F conventional oven 35–40 minutes. Makes 6 servings.

Sheila Mills, *The Outdoor Dutch Oven Cookbook*

Mom's Tuna-Noodle Casserole

1 T. vegetable oil
1 small can tuna, drained
1 c. egg noodles, cooked
1 packet (single-serving size) mushroom soup mix, and water
    to prepare
$1/4$ c. parsley, chopped
1 T. margarine, melted
bread crumbs

In lightly greased baking pan, mix tuna, noodles, soup, and parsley. Drizzle margarine over top. Sprinkle bread crumbs over all. Bake 35 minutes in medium oven.

Don Jacobson, *The One Pan Gourmet*

CHICKEN

Baked Wheat Germ Chicken

1 large, three-drumstick frying chicken
1/2 c. (1 stick) butter, melted
1 c. wheat germ
salt and pepper to taste
paprika to taste

Skin and dry chicken pieces. Roll each in melted butter and then dip into wheat germ to coat. Place pieces in a Dutch oven or baking dish. Pour remaining butter over chicken and season with salt and pepper. Garnish with paprika.

Bake 40–45 minutes in the Dutch oven, or 45–50 minutes in a 350°F conventional oven. Makes 4–6 servings.

Sheila Mills, *The Outdoor Dutch Oven Cookbook*

Sticky Chicken

1 jar (8 oz.) apricot or pineapple jam
1/2 envelope dry Lipton onion soup mix
1 bottle (8 oz.) spicy French salad dressing
1 large chicken, cut into eight pieces
salt and pepper to taste

Mix together jam, dry soup, and salad dressing. Chill 1 hour or longer to blend the flavors. Place chicken parts in a Dutch oven or 2-quart casserole dish and pour sauce over them. Season with salt and pepper to taste.

Bake in Dutch oven 45–50 minutes, or covered in 350°F conventional oven 50–60 minutes, or until tender. Makes 6 servings.

Sheila Mills, *The Outdoor Dutch Oven Cookbook*

Mom's Famous Casserole

12 oz. wide egg noodles, cooked
2 c. diced, cooked chicken or turkey
1 can (10 1/2 oz.) cream of mushroom soup
2 large bunches of broccoli, cut into chunks
4 oz. (1 c.) Cheddar cheese, grated
mayonnaise, if needed to moisten

Combine all ingredients in a Dutch oven or 1 1/2-quart casserole dish.

Bake in Dutch oven 30–40 minutes, or in 350°F conventional oven 40–45 minutes. Makes 6 servings.

Sheila Mills, *The Outdoor Dutch Oven Cookbook*

BBC (Basic Baked Chicken)

1/2 lb. chicken (white or dark pieces)
1 medium onion, sliced
1 stalk celery, chopped
1 carrot, cut in strips
1 medium potato, cut in chunks
salt and pepper to taste

Place chicken in baking pan and surround with vegetables. Add salt and pepper. Bake about 45 minutes in medium oven. Serve with a hard roll and fruit.

Don Jacobson, *The One Pan Gourmet*

"Pardon Me, but Do You Have Any . . . " Chicken

1 clove garlic, minced
2 T. Dijon mustard
1/4 t. thyme
salt and pepper to taste
2 chicken breast halves, boned (with skin)

Mix garlic with mustard, thyme, salt, and pepper. Remove skin gently from meat and rub mixture on chicken. Replace skin. Salt and pepper again. Place chicken in baking pan and bake 35–40 minutes in medium oven on low rack. If you like, cut a potato in half, wrap it in foil, and bake it on the higher rack.

Don Jacobson, *The One Pan Gourmet*

Crumby Chicken

$1/4$ c. Parmesan cheese
$1/2$ c. seasoned bread crumbs
$1/2$ lb. chicken (white or dark pieces)
$1/4$ c. milk
1 yellow squash or zucchini, cut in 1-inch slices

Mix cheese and bread crumbs together. Dip chicken in milk and roll in coating mix. Place in baking pan. Dip squash in milk and then in coating mix. Arrange vegetables on top of chicken. Bake in medium oven 45 minutes.

Don Jacobson, *The One Pan Gourmet*

Cheesy Chicken

$1/2$ c. milk
$1/2$ c. Monterey Jack cheese, shredded
$1/2$ lb. chicken breast, cooked and diced
1 c. cooked macaroni
1 sweet red pepper, diced
seasoned bread crumbs

Over medium flame, heat milk to almost boiling. Slowly add cheese and stir until smooth. In oven pan, combine chicken, macaroni, and red pepper. Pour cheese sauce over top. Sprinkle with bread crumbs. Bake in a medium oven 25 minutes.

Don Jacobson, *The One Pan Gourmet*

Divine Chicken

1 chicken breast half, boned
$3/4$ c. broccoli
1 packet (single-serving size) mushroom soup mix, reconstituted

Place chicken breast in baking pan and cover with broccoli. Pour mushroom soup over all. Cover and bake in medium oven 35–40 minutes.

Don Jacobson, *The One Pan Gourmet*

OTHER MEATS

Ham 'n' Cheese Spuds

3 medium potatoes, sliced thin
4 oz. ham, diced (optional)
$1/3$ c. Cheddar cheese, grated
1 medium onion, sliced thin
$3/4$ c. milk
2 T. flour
salt and pepper to taste

In baking pan, layer potatoes with ham, cheese, and onion. Combine milk, flour, salt, and pepper. Pour over mixture in pan. Bake in medium oven 45 minutes.

Don Jacobson, *The One Pan Gourmet*

Shepherd's Pie

2 large potatoes, peeled and sliced thin
2 T. butter or margarine
$1/4$ c. milk
$1/2$ lb. ground beef
salt and pepper to taste
2 T. flour
$1/4$ c. water
2 carrots, chopped
1 stalk celery, chopped
1 medium onion, chopped

Boil potatoes in salted water 15 minutes, using your oven pan as a pot. Drain water. Mash potatoes with butter and milk. Remove from pan and set aside. Clean pan. Over medium flame, brown ground beef until crumbly. Reduce heat and add salt, pepper, flour, and water. Stir to make gravy. Remove from heat. Add vegetables to pot and stir to mix. Make crust of mashed potatoes over the top of the meat-and-vegetable mixture. Bake 35 minutes in medium oven.

Don Jacobson, *The One Pan Gourmet*

Champignon Chops

2 center-cut loin pork chops, boned
1 packet (single-serving size) mushroom soup mix,
    reconstituted
parsley, chopped
1 large potato, sliced

In baking pan, brown chops in a little oil. Remove from
heat and pour mushroom soup over top. Sprinkle with parsley.
Arrange potato slices around edge of pan. Cover and bake
45 minutes in medium oven.

Don Jacobson, *The One Pan Gourmet*

Big BBQ Ribs

2 farmer-style (i.e., with meat on, not spare ribs) pork ribs
$1/2$ c. BBQ sauce
1 medium onion, cut in chunks
1 c. rice, cooked

Place ribs in baking pan and smother with BBQ sauce. Pack
onion pieces around ribs. Bake in medium oven 45 minutes to
1 hour. About 10 minutes before ribs are done, add rice.

Don Jacobson, *The One Pan Gourmet*

Complete Meal Muffins

2 c. canned corned beef
2 c. soft bread crumbs
2 extra-large eggs
2 T. packed brown sugar
1 T. mustard powder
2 T. water

Combine all ingredients and bake in greased muffin tins at
300°F for 35 minutes. Makes 4–6 servings.

Jean and Samuel Spangenberg, *The Portable Baker*

VEGGIE DISHES

Field-Tested Pizza

3–4 c. water
$1/2$ recipe dried All-Around Tomato Sauce (see recipe
   page 117) or 2 cans (15 oz. ea.) tomato sauce with
   Italian spices, dried
$1/2$ c. dried mushrooms
1 dried pepper
1 dried onion
1 bannock mix (see recipe page 52)
warm water
$1/3$ lb. mozzarella cheese, thinly sliced

Boil water in a saucepan and divide between two bowls, using
to rehydrate tomato sauce in one bowl (enough water for a fairly
thick paste), and the veggies in the other.

Mix dribbles of warm water with bannock mix until slightly
sticky. Flatten dough evenly in the bottom of a 10- or 12-inch-
diameter, lightly oiled pan (Dutch oven or heavy-gauge metal).
Cook one side of dough over low heat until just barely browned,
turn uncooked side down, and remove pan from heat.

Make an attractive layering with half the mozzarella, sauce,
then drained veggies sprinkled over so everyone gets the same
goodies on each piece. Finally, add remaining mozzarella.

If cooking with a Dutch oven over a fire, scrape coals from the
fire pit and place the Dutch oven on the bare, hot ground (a very
thin coal layer is OK). Use a trowel to heap hot coals on the lid
and let the pizza bake until your site smells like a pizzeria. For
stove-top cooking, set heat at very low flame, brown *both* sides
of the crust first, then cover, and check until it looks done. (A little
sprinkling of water dashed on top can help steam the pizza.)

Toppings of your choice—black olives, pineapple, sliced
sausage, or whatever, vary the flavor and texture.

Alan Kesselheim, *Trail Food*

Black Bean Burritos

12 flour tortillas, 10-inch diameter
3 c. canned black beans, drained
$1^1/_2$ c. finely chopped red onion
3 c. grated Monterey Jack cheese
3 avocados, peeled, pitted, and cut into chunks
6 T. chopped cilantro
1 c. salsa

Working with one tortilla at a time, spread $^1/_4$ cup of the black beans in the center. Top beans with 1 tablespoon onion and $^1/_4$ cup of the Monterey Jack. Roll tortilla gently to enclose filling. Repeat for remaining tortillas. Transfer burritos, seam sides down, to a Dutch oven or 9-by-12-inch baking pan, forming one layer.

Bake in Dutch oven 15–20 minutes, or in 350°F conventional oven 15–20 minutes. Top each burrito with avocado, cilantro, and salsa. Makes 12 servings.

Sheila Mills, *The Outdoor Dutch Oven Cookbook*

Italian Zucchini Bake

1 T. olive oil
$^1/_2$ c. chopped onion
3 c. shredded zucchini (squeeze out all excess moisture)
$1^1/_4$ c. rolled oats
1 oz. mozzarella cheese, grated ($^1/_4$ c.)
1 egg
$^1/_2$ t. dried basil, crushed
$^1/_2$ t. salt (optional)
$^1/_4$ t. freshly ground pepper
$^1/_3$ c. tomato sauce

Heat olive oil in 10-inch Dutch oven or skillet, add onion, and sauté until tender. Transfer onion to large bowl and add remaining ingredients except tomato sauce. Mix well. Pour mixture into Dutch oven or $1^1/_2$-quart casserole dish. Spread tomato sauce evenly over the top.

Bake in Dutch oven 30 minutes, or in 350°F conventional oven 30 minutes. Makes 6–8 servings.

Sheila Mills, *The Outdoor Dutch Oven Cookbook*

Real Men Eat Dutch Oven Quiche

1 c. dried veggies of choice (zucchini, onion, carrot, and/or tomato)
enough warm water (about 2 c.) to rehydrate veggies
1 bannock mix (page 52)
3 T. water
$1/2$ c. butter, margarine, or oil (butter is best)
4 dried eggs (see recipe page 16), reconstituted in 1 c. water
$1 1/2$ c. milk
2 T. flour
1 t. dry mustard
salt and pepper to taste
1 clove fresh garlic, minced
$1/2$ t. tarragon
$1/2$ lb. cheese (Swiss-Cheddar mix is good)
paprika

Start rehydrating your veggies on the side while you tackle the crust. Combine bannock mix, water, and fat until dough is just slightly sticky. Oil the bottom of a 10- or 12-inch-diameter Dutch oven, and press out the crust evenly with your fingers (or use a smooth-sided cup as a rolling pin). Set aside.

Next, mix eggs, milk, flour, and seasonings (except paprika) in a bowl and let sit.

Slice half the cheese thinly and spread over the crust. When veggies are tender, drain excess water and spread atop the cheese. Pour the liquid filling evenly over veggies. Slice the rest of the cheese and lay it decoratively over all. Finish off with a sprinkling of paprika.

Bake under coals 30–45 minutes, or until you smell the baked crust. When quiche is done, it will barely jiggle. If it still dances, continue baking.

Variations:

- sun-dried tomatoes or dried Oriental mushrooms are great quiche ingredients

- dill is another quichey seasoning, and either parsley or cilantro makes a tasty addition

Alan Kesselheim, *Trail Food*

Ah-Hoooaa! Enchilada Bake

1 large onion, dried
1 pkg. (10 oz.) frozen, chopped spinach, dried
water to rehydrate veggies
3 cloves fresh garlic, minced
1 can (10 oz.) enchilada sauce (can be dried and then
  rehydrated in the field)
12 small corn tortillas
8 oz. cottage cheese
1/2 lb. Monterey Jack cheese, sliced thin

Heat water and rehydrate onion and spinach with garlic (and enchilada sauce in another bowl, if necessary). Briefly heat both sides of the tortillas in a lightly oiled pan and set aside. Mix cottage cheese with spinach mixture.

To assemble, spoon a small amount of enchilada sauce on the bottom of a Dutch oven or heavy pot. Alternate layers of tortilla, cottage cheese–spinach, and Monterey Jack until you use it all up. Finish by pouring enchilada sauce evenly over the top and sprinkling any extra cheese over the sauce.

Simmer over very low heat (or, better yet, bake under coals) until the enchilada is bubbly, melted, and ready to assault the taste buds.

Variations:

- black olives are good in the cottage cheese–spinach mix
- dried refried beans, rehydrated and spooned on between layers, make a heartier dish
- cilantro adds interesting flavor

Alan Kesselheim, *Trail Food*

Crustless Spinach Pie

1 pkg. (10 oz.) frozen chopped spinach or broccoli,
  thawed and well drained (or fresh, cooked, well
  drained, and chopped)
1/2 lb. sharp Cheddar or feta cheese, grated or crumbled
2 c. low-fat cottage cheese
4 eggs
6 T. flour
1/4 t. salt
1/2 t. pepper

In a bowl, combine spinach, grated cheese, and cottage cheese. In a cup, mix eggs with a fork and add flour, salt, and pepper. Combine both mixtures and mix well. Place mixture in a lightly oiled or nonstick pie pan, and bake 1 hour in medium oven.

Don Jacobson, *The One Pan Gourmet*

Delicious Scalloped Potatoes

3 c. sliced onion
2 T. olive oil
3 lb. boiling potatoes (white, rose or red skinned),
    peeled and sliced
$1^1/_2$ c. milk
1 clove garlic, finely chopped
$1/_4$ t. Italian herbs
salt and pepper

Sauté onions in olive oil until soft. In a 9-by-13-inch oiled baking dish, layer potatoes and onions. Cover with remaining ingredients. Bake at 400°F for 40 minutes. Makes 6–8 servings.

Kay Pastorius, *Cruising Cuisine*

John Barley Cake

$1/_4$ c. flour
$1^1/_4$ c. water
$1/_2$ c. barley, raw
1 medium onion, diced
1 medium zucchini, diced
$1/_2$ T. vegetable oil
$1/_4$ t. salt (optional)
$1/_4$ t. oregano

Mix flour with $3/_4$ cup of the water; stir to remove lumps. Combine with remaining ingredients (including remaining $1/_2$ cup water) in baking pan. Cook in medium oven 30 minutes, or until water is absorbed and top is firm.

Don Jacobson, *The One Pan Gourmet*

It's true what they say: food—even the ordinary—always tastes better at camp. And no meal is better than dinner after a big day. So, if camp cooks could get away with the ordinary, why bother finding new recipes, putting so much care into pre-trip preparation, and now—after weathering a full day's adventures—gearing up to prepare a feast for a ravenous crowd? Because it's the big reward!

THE RECIPES IN THIS SECTION include a variety of field-tested skillet winners, including meat and fish entrées, a healthy selection of vegetarian options, and light meals that can stand on their own or—for really hungry campers—serve as appetizers. You'll also find under the Sauces and Mixtures heading a few concoctions that don't fit neatly into other categories.

(continued from previous page)

CHICKEN

Walnut Chicken

1/4 c. vegetable oil
1 c. walnuts
1 T. cornstarch
2 T. cold water
2 T. soy sauce
2 boneless chicken breast halves
1 chicken bouillon cube
3/4 c. boiling water
1 t. salt (optional)
1 c. cooked rice

Heat oil in frying pan over high heat. Sauté walnuts lightly (do not brown). Remove walnuts and reserve oil. Mix cornstarch, cold water, and soy sauce with 3 tablespoons of reserved oil. Pour into hot pan; add chicken and brown. Add slices of green pepper, if you like.

Dissolve bouillon cube in boiling water; add to pan. Stir in salt (if desired) and walnuts. Stir until thick and serve over cooked rice.

Don Jacobson, *The One Pan Gourmet*

Delhi Chicken with Rice

1 T. vegetable oil
1 medium onion, chopped
2 boneless chicken breast halves, cut in 1-inch cubes
1 T. flour
1/4 t. ginger
1–2 T. curry powder (or to taste)
2 T. honey
2 T. soy sauce
2 chicken bouillon cubes
2 c. water
3/4 c. white rice, uncooked
1–2 carrots, sliced

Heat oil in pan. Add onion and sauté until brown. Add chicken and brown. Sprinkle flour, ginger, and curry powder into pan and stir. Add honey, soy sauce, bouillon cubes, and water. Simmer 5 minutes. Add rice and carrots. Stir and simmer uncovered for another 20–25 minutes.

Don Jacobson, *The One Pan Gourmet*

Mr. Natural's Fried Fowl

2 eggs
$1/2$ c. milk
$1/4$ c. flour
$1/2$ c. granola, oatmeal, or other grain
salt and pepper to taste
$1/2$ lb. chicken (white or dark pieces)
$1/2$ c. peanut oil

Mix eggs, milk, flour, and grain together. If batter seems thin, add more flour. Rub salt and pepper on chicken and then dip it into batter. Heat pan and add oil. When oil bubbles, place chicken in pan and cook thoroughly, turning periodically until tender. Remove chicken to drain on paper towel.

Don Jacobson, *The One Pan Gourmet*

Icebox Chicken with Stuffing

3 T. margarine
1 medium onion, diced
$1/2$ c. green pepper, chopped
1 small tomato, diced
1 stalk celery, chopped
$1/2$ lb. boneless chicken breast, cubed
salt and pepper to taste
1 chicken bouillon cube
$1/2$ c. water
$1/2$ c. seasoned croutons, stuffing mix, or instant rice
$1/2$ t. poultry seasoning if you use instant rice

Over a medium flame, heat pot. Melt margarine in pot and sauté vegetables until tender. Add chicken and cook until meat is done. Add salt and pepper, bouillon cube, and water. Continue cooking until cube is dissolved. Add croutons and stir until liquid is absorbed and croutons are soft. If you substitute instant rice for croutons, cover the pot and let it stand off the heat a few minutes. Cooking time will vary depending on the stove and altitude.

Don Jacobson, *The One Pan Gourmet*

Chicken 'n' Green-Eyed Gravy

1 T. vegetable oil
2 boneless chicken breast halves, cut in chunks
1 medium onion, chopped
3/4 c. water
1 chicken bouillon cube
3/4 c. freeze-dried or dehydrated peas
salt and pepper to taste
flour and water to thicken

Heat pot over medium flame. Add oil and brown chicken. Add onion and cook until soft. Add all other ingredients except flour and cook about 30 minutes or until peas are soft. Add water as needed. Thicken gravy by making paste of water and flour and stirring in gradually to prevent lumps.

Don Jacobson, *The One Pan Gourmet*

Creamed Chicken and Noodles

2 chicken bouillon cubes
1 1/2 c. water
1 boneless chicken breast half, cut in chunks
3 oz. cream cheese
1/2 c. freeze-dried or dehydrated peas
2 T. flour
1 red pepper, diced
1 c. cooked noodles or macaroni

In pot, bring bouillon cubes and water to boil. Add all other ingredients except noodles (add cheese a chunk at a time). Reduce heat, cover, and simmer 30 minutes. Stir occasionally. Serve over cooked noodles.

Don Jacobson, *The One Pan Gourmet*

Skillet Dinners

OTHER MEATS

Burritos

1 lb. ground beef
1 onion, chopped
1 can (16 oz.) refried beans
1 can (15 oz.) diced tomatoes
1 c. salsa of choice
small head lettuce (or 1 bag prepared)
1 can medium black olives, sliced in half
jalapeno peppers (optional)
1 pkg. (16 oz.) shredded Cheddar cheese
1 pkg. thick flour tortillas (10–12)

Sauté ground beef and half the onion in a skillet; drain excess fat. Add beans, tomatoes, half the salsa, and simmer. Set out lettuce, sliced olives, remaining onion, remaining salsa, and cheese. Grab a tortilla and pile on the fillings, roll it up, and eat. Then do it all over again! Serves 5–6.

Hamburger Hash

$1/2$ lb. ground beef
$1/2$ medium onion, diced
$1/2$ c. pinto beans (previously soaked and packed in plastic bag)
2 oz. ketchup
1 T. brown sugar
$1/2$ c. water
1 beef bouillon cube
salt and pepper to taste

Brown beef and add onion. Cook until tender. Add all remaining ingredients. Stir mixture and simmer 10–15 minutes or until sauce is smooth.

Don Jacobson, *The One Pan Gourmet*

Cajun-Style Blackened Fish

4 fish fillets, $1/2$ inch thick
2–4 T. cooking oil

Cajun Spice Mixture:
1 T. paprika
2 t. garlic powder
1 t. ground cayenne pepper
1 t. ground black pepper
1 t. ground white pepper
$1/2$ t. salt
$1/2$ t. dried oregano
$1/2$ t. dried thyme

Mix together the ingredients of the Cajun Spice Mixture (pre-mixed Cajun spices are available commercially, but they're often very salty). The spices can be combined in advance and stored in a sealed container.

If using a propane barbecue, heat skillet on the highest setting for 10 minutes. If using briquettes, allow the coals to burn down and place the skillet as close to coals as possible; allow to heat at least 10 minutes.

Coat each fillet with Cajun Spice Mixture.

Pour oil in the skillet and *carefully* place the fillets in the hot oil. Cook approximately 3–4 minutes before turning fish. Add more oil if necessary. The object is to seal in the juices by searing fish on a very hot fire and cooking until barely done.

To reduce the spiciness of Cajun Spice Mixture, add dry bread crumbs to suit your taste. For very thin fillets ($1/8$ inch thick), you can use half bread crumbs and half Cajun Spice Mixture.

Makes 4 servings.

Kay Pastorius, *Cruising Cuisine*

Soupy Meatballs

$1/2$ lb. ground beef
$1/4$ c. seasoned bread crumbs
$1/2$ medium onion, diced
salt and pepper to taste
2 T. corn oil
1 c. water
1 packet (single-serving size) beef-based soup mix

Combine meat, bread crumbs, onion, salt, and pepper. Shape into small meatballs (1–1$1/2$ inches in diameter). Heat frying pan and add oil. Brown meatballs, rolling them around to brown evenly. Add water and soup mix. Simmer 5–10 minutes. If desired, add thinly sliced potato (unpeeled) or other veggies to bubbling mix and cook until done.

Don Jacobson, *The One Pan Gourmet*

Hair-Raisin Curry Beef

$1/2$ c. boiling water
$1/2$ c. raisins
1 T. olive oil
$1/2$ lb. sirloin, cut in 1-inch cubes
$1/2$ medium onion, chopped
$1/2$ medium green pepper, chopped
$1/2$ T. curry powder
$1/2$ t. salt (optional)
$1/3$ c. unsalted peanuts
1 beef bouillon cube

In a dish or small bowl, pour boiling water over raisins and set aside. In a frying pan, add oil and brown meat and vegetables over medium heat. Drain oil. Add curry powder and mix well. Mix in salt (if desired) and nuts. Drain raisins (reserve juice); add raisins to meat mixture. To reserved raisin juice, add enough water to measure $1/2$ cup. Add this and bouillon cube to meat mixture and simmer 15 minutes.

Don Jacobson, *The One Pan Gourmet*

Tokyo Teriyaki

$1/2$ lb. sirloin steak, cut in 1-inch cubes
$1/3$ medium onion, chopped
$1/4$ t. ginger
2 oz. teriyaki sauce
$1/2$–1 c. cooked rice
pineapple chunks

Combine steak, onion, ginger, and teriyaki sauce in bowl and marinate 10–15 minutes. Heat frying pan and add steak and marinade. Cook until done, adding a little water if necessary. Push meat and onions to one side of pan. Add cooked rice and heat through. About 1 minute before serving, add and heat pineapple chunks.

Don Jacobson, *The One Pan Gourmet*

Soy Sauce Sirloin

$1/4$ c. peanut oil
6 oz. sirloin, sliced thin
3 green onions, sliced in 1-inch pieces
1 can (6 oz.) water chestnuts, sliced
1 medium green pepper, sliced
2 oz. dried pineapple chunks
2 T. cornstarch
$1/4$ c. water
$1/4$ c. soy sauce

Preheat pan and add oil. Sauté beef in hot oil about 30 seconds on each side. Add remaining ingredients except cornstarch, water, and soy sauce. Cook 4–5 minutes over medium flame. Meanwhile, dissolve cornstarch in water. Add cornstarch mixture and soy sauce to pan and stir until thickened.

Don Jacobson, *The One Pan Gourmet*

Creamed Corned Beef and Cabbage

1 small cabbage, shredded
$1/2$ t. salt
$1/2$ c. water
1 c. milk (or $1/3$ c. dried milk reconstituted in 1 c. water)
1 T. flour or instant potato
1 can (12 oz.) corned beef, broken into small pieces

Simmer cabbage in salted water until done. Drain. Pour milk over cabbage. When hot, stir in flour and corned beef. Reheat. Serves 3–4.

Harriett Barker, *The One-Burner Gourmet*

Big Mo Chops

2 center-cut pork loin chops, thick cut
1 medium onion, sliced
1 medium green pepper, cut in strips
1 large potato, sliced
3 deli packets ketchup (or 1 T.)
2 T. molasses
2 T. water

In pot over medium flame, brown chops. Remove from pot and drain off fat. Add onion to pot. Lay meat on onion, and other vegetables on top of meat. Cover with ketchup and molasses. Drizzle water over top. Cover and cook 40 minutes over low heat. Add additional water if sauce is too thick.

Don Jacobson, *The One Pan Gourmet*

VEGGIE DISHES

One More Time Mac 'n' Cheese

3 T. dried tomato sauce (with enough water to rehydrate)
1 t. dill
salt and pepper to taste
2 qt. water
1 dried onion
$1/2$ c. dried peas
1 T. oil
4 c. veggie spiral noodles
$1/3$ c. dried milk
$1/3$ lb. Cheddar cheese, cubed
3 T. margarine

You may tire of other meals, but this old standby will keep making the menu list, trip after trip. Start by reconstituting the tomato sauce with just enough water to make a paste, along with the seasonings. Meanwhile, boil the onion and peas in the water until peas are nearly cooked. Stir in oil and noodles. When noodles are *al dente*, drain most of the water (leaving enough to reconstitute milk, about ½ cup). Return to low heat and add reconstituted tomato sauce, milk, cheese, and margarine. Stir frequently until ingredients are well mixed and cheese is melted.

Alan Kesselheim, *Trail Food*

Curried Rice and Veggies

$31/2$ c. water
1 c. dried veggie mix (see recipe page 117)
1 c. white basmati rice
3–4 T. margarine
$1/2$ c. chopped almonds or cashews
$1/2$ c. raisins
2 T. curry powder (or to taste)

Boil water and veggie mix 5–10 minutes, then add rice and cover. Simmer until rice is cooked, veggies are tender, and water is nearly gone (15–20 minutes).

When the rice is almost cooked, melt margarine in large frying pan or Dutch oven. Sauté nuts and raisins, adding curry and stirring so everything is coated nicely. Stir in rice and veggies and cook, stirring, a few more minutes.

Alan Kesselheim, *Trail Food*

SOUR CREAM MIX

Many grocery stores sell packaged sour cream mix. You'll probably find the envelopes shelved with salad dressings. Dehydrating your own is a lot cheaper, but you can also purchase sour cream powder in bulk from Adventure Foods at www.adventurefoods.com.

Cheesy, Spicy Beans and Ricey

4 c. water
$1/2$ c. black-eyed peas
1 can (4 oz.) green chilis, dried (about $1/4$ c.)
1 dried onion
1 c. white basmati rice
4 T. dried salsa, rehydrated in 1 c. warm water
3 cloves fresh garlic, minced (or powder to taste)
1 t. salt
pinch cumin
1 envelope sour cream mix
$1/2$ lb. Monterey Jack cheese, cubed

Add peas, chilis, and onion to boiling water and cook until peas start to soften (20 minutes). Add rice, cover, and simmer until done (another 15 minutes). Drain any excess water.

Meantime, rehydrate salsa with minced garlic and other spices, and prepare the sour cream in a cup. When rice is done, mix everything but the sour cream together and bake briefly (if using fire), or heat on low flame until cheese melts and flavors meld. Garnish with sour cream.

Alan Kesselheim, *Trail Food*

Spaghetti Night!

1/2 recipe All-Around Tomato Sauce (page 117), dried,
    or 2 cans (15 oz. ea.) tomato sauce simmered
    with Italian spices, dried
1 c. dried veggie mix (see recipe page 117)
6–8 c. water
1 t. oil or margarine
1/2 lb. spaghetti
1/2 c. grated Parmesan cheese (optional)

Rehydrate sauce, adding boiling water until sauce is of the desired consistency. Simmer until the flavor is perfect for you, adding more spices if necessary. Add dried veggies and more water. While the sauce bubbles, boil water in large pot, add oil and spaghetti, and stir a few times. When pasta is done (10 minutes), drain and mix in the sauce. Sprinkle liberally with Parmesan cheese, if desired.

Variations:

*   try spinach or artichoke pasta
*   try garlic-parsley ribbon noodles for variety

Alan Kesselheim, *Trail Food*

Spinach and Rice Feast

1/2 lb. fresh spinach, chopped and dried
1 lb. ground beef, sautéed and dried
1 onion (fresh or dried)
1 veggie bouillon cube
2 c. water
salt and pepper, to taste
2 c. cooked brown rice
small container yogurt (optional)

This is a tasty variation on a traditional Turkish dinner. Combine all ingredients except rice and yogurt in a pot. Simmer until rehydrated and well blended (add more water if desired). Cook rice separately. Serve spinach-beef mix over the rice. A yogurt topping is a nice touch, if you can bring it along.

Alan Kesselheim, *Trail Food*

Mushroom-Cauliflower Hot Dish

4–5 c. water
1/3 c. dried mushrooms
1 small head cauliflower, dried
1 large dried onion
1 c. white basmati rice
2 cloves garlic, minced
1 t. basil
1 T. grated lemon rind (optional)
salt and pepper to taste
1/3 lb. Cheddar cheese, cubed small

Bring water to a boil with the dried veggies. Simmer 10 minutes, then add rice and cover. When rice is cooked, pour off excess water and add remaining ingredients. Heat long enough to melt cheese and blend seasonings, or bake 15 minutes in Dutch oven.

Alan Kesselheim, *Trail Food*

Chuck's Pesto Fiesta

6–8 c. water
1/2 lb. spaghetti or 4 c. veggie spirals
1/4 c. olive oil
2 T. melted butter
1/2 c. sun-dried or dehydrated tomatoes
1/2 c. Oriental dried mushrooms
1/2 dried pesto recipe (page 116) (packaged dried pesto
    can be bought at gourmet grocers)
grated Parmesan cheese (optional)

Boil water and add spaghetti. While the pasta is cooking, heat the oil and butter in a large pan and add tomatoes and mushrooms to sauté a bit. Then add the dried pesto powder and sauté until it thickens nicely (a T. of water may be necessary).

Right about now the pasta will be done, so drain the water off and stir in the pesto and veggies. Serve right away, and pass the Parmesan, please.

Alan Kesselheim, *Trail Food*

Spanish Bulgur

4–5 c. water
1 can (4 oz.) green chilis, dried (about 1/4 c.)
2 dried onions
1 dried green pepper
2 dried tomatoes
1/3 c. black-eyed peas
1 brimming c. bulgur
1 t. salt
1/2 t. oregano
1/2 t. basil
dash of garlic
1 T. chili powder
pinch of cumin
1/3 lb. Monterey Jack cheese, cubed

Boil dried veggies and black-eyed peas in the water. When peas are nearly cooked (20–30 minutes), add bulgur and all seasonings. When all is soft, juicy, and mouthwatering, throw in the cheese and heat until it's melted in.

Alan Kesselheim, *Trail Food*

Sunshine Squash

2 T. peanut oil
1 medium onion, diced
1 medium summer squash, diced
5 or 6 mushrooms, sliced or chopped
1/4–1/2 t. garlic powder
1/4 t. pepper
salt to taste

Preheat frying pan over medium flame. Add oil and sauté onion until tender. Add squash and cook uncovered until desired tenderness (I like mine "crisp-tender"). Add mushrooms and seasonings and cook 3–4 more minutes.

Don Jacobson, *The One Pan Gourmet*

Tasty Pasta with Cheese

    4 oz. pasta (2 good handfuls), uncooked
    1 T. olive oil
    1 t. vegetable oil
    $1/4$ t. hot pepper flakes
    salt and pepper to taste
    1 handful shelled walnuts or pine nuts
    $1/4$ c. any grated cheese

In salted boiling water, cook pasta until done. Drain and return to pot. Add remaining ingredients. Gently toss.

Don Jacobson, *The One Pan Gourmet*

Zucchini in Tomato Sauce

    5 tomatoes
    $1/4$ c. margarine (½ stick)
    $1/2$ t. salt
    dash of pepper
    $1/2$ t. basil
    1 lb. zucchini, washed and sliced thin
    1 t. dry parsley flakes

Peel (optional) and cut up tomatoes. Sauté in margarine in large frying pan or 2-quart pot, stirring constantly until thick. Add seasonings and sliced zucchini. Simmer 12–15 minutes. Sprinkle with parsley flakes and stir lightly. Serves 4–5.

Harriett Barker, *The One-Burner Gourmet*

FOIL MEALS

Foil Dinner

1 hamburger patty
1 potato, peeled or scrubbed and cubed
1 carrot, peeled or scrubbed and cut in strips
1 onion, peeled and cut in wedges
salt and pepper

This is a delicious and easy-to-make meal. Place a hamburger patty on a large piece of heavy-duty aluminum foil. Cover hamburger with vegetables. Sprinkle with salt and pepper to taste.

Fold foil over and close it securely to make a small, tight package. Place package in coals and cook 15–30 minutes, depending on the temperature of the coals. Makes 1 serving.

Victoria Logue, Frank Logue, and Mark Carroll, *Kids Outdoors*

Foil-Baked Fish

filleted fish
salt and pepper to taste
onion, sliced into rings
lemon, sliced
tomato, sliced

Lay out a strip of heavy-duty aluminum foil and butter generously. Lay out a filleted fish on the foil. Sprinkle with salt and pepper. Cover with onion rings, lemon slices, tomato slices. Seal tightly with foil and place on a grill over the coals. When steam balloons the foil, prick it once to release the steam. A large filleted fish cooks in 20–30 minutes.

Chef's secret: If you use fish that tends to be dry, add a can of tomato sauce.

Harriett Barker, *The One-Burner Gourmet*

SEALING FOIL MEALS

Use a **drugstore wrap** to seal foil meals: Bring two sides of the foil together, fold down in a series of folds, and flatten. Fold the ends toward the center in tight folds to seal the package.

Foil-Wrapped Chicken with Salsa

1 whole chicken, cut into serving pieces
1 t. chopped garlic
1 can (4 oz.) chunky salsa
1 onion, chopped
1 c. chopped celery

Place chicken pieces on a large piece of heavy-duty aluminum foil and cover with remaining ingredients. Wrap tightly and marinate 30 minutes.

Bake over hot coals 35–45 minutes. Serve warm, using the juices from the foil as a sauce. Makes 4 servings.

Kay Pastorius, *Cruising Cuisine*

Foil-Wrapped Veggie Pack

1 tomato, chopped
2 carrots, chopped
1 potato, chopped
1 onion, peeled and chopped
2 cloves garlic, finely chopped
2 T. fresh or canned pesto sauce
3 T. white wine

Place vegetables in the center of a rectangular piece of heavy-duty aluminum foil and sprinkle with remaining ingredients. Seal the package.

Place on a preheated barbecue. Cook until package puffs up and is hot on top—about 30 minutes. Makes 2 servings.

Kay Pastorius, *Cruising Cuisine*

Trout 'n' Apple

8 small to medium trout, cleaned
3 cooking apples, peeled, cored, and chopped fine
cinnamon to taste

Place the cleaned fish on heavy-duty foil. Top with chopped apples and a dash or two of cinnamon. Wrap foil to seal securely, place on coals, and add a cover of coals. Leave for 30–45 minutes, depending on size of fish. Serves 4–5.

Harriett Barker, *The One-Burner Gourmet*

Garlic Potatoes

4 red skinned potatoes, thinly sliced
3 T. olive oil
2 t. Lawry's Lemon Pepper Seasoning
8 cloves garlic, finely chopped

Dip each potato slice in olive oil and sprinkle with lemon pepper and garlic. Spread on a piece of heavy-duty foil and seal foil. Cook on the barbecue about 10–15 minutes or until the foil is hot to the touch on top and you can hear the oil sizzling inside. If you like crispier potatoes, open the foil for the last 5 minutes of cooking. Makes 2 servings.

Kay Pastorius, *Cruising Cuisine*

LIGHT ENTRÉES

Barley and Wild Rice

1 onion, chopped
2 cloves garlic, finely chopped
1 c. pearl barley
1/2 c. wild rice
1 T. olive oil
4 c. water
2 t. salt

Sauté onion, garlic, barley, and rice in oil until onion is soft.
Add water and salt and bring to a boil. Cover and simmer until the grains are tender and the water is absorbed—about 1 hour. Makes 4–6 servings.

Kay Pastorius, *Cruising Cuisine*

Red Rice

1 small onion, chopped
1 clove garlic, minced
2 T. olive oil
1 1/2 c. long-grain white rice
2 c. beef broth
1/2 t. salt
1 c. (8 fluid oz.) tomato sauce

In a saucepan, sauté onion and garlic in olive oil until tender. Stir in rice and sauté 3–5 minutes longer, stirring until all the grains of rice are coated with a little oil.

Add remaining ingredients and bring to a boil. Reduce heat, cover, and simmer 20–25 minutes until rice is tender. Makes 6–8 servings.

Kay Pastorius, *Cruising Cuisine*

Curried Cauliflower

2 T. chopped fresh ginger
1 onion, chopped
2 t. curry powder
2 T. cooking oil
1 lb. cauliflower, cut in 1 1/2-inch pieces
2 potatoes, finely chopped
1/2 t. salt
1/4 c. water

Sauté ginger, onion, and curry powder in oil for 3 minutes. Add remaining ingredients, cover pan, and cook until vegetables are soft—about 20 minutes. Add more water if the vegetables start to stick to the pan. Makes 4 servings.

Kay Pastorius, *Cruising Cuisine*

Stir-Fried Spicy Cabbage

2 T. sugar
2 T. rice wine vinegar
1 T. soy sauce
1 t. salt
1/4 t. cayenne pepper
1 T. cooking oil
3/4 lb. napa cabbage, cut into 1-inch squares

Make a sauce by combining sugar, wine vinegar, soy sauce, salt, and cayenne pepper; set aside. Heat a wok, add oil, and heat. Add cabbage and stir-fry 2 minutes, making sure the cabbage is evenly coated with oil. Remove wok from heat and stir in sauce. Serve warm or cold. Makes 4 servings.

Kay Pastorius, *Cruising Cuisine*

McAuliffe's Green Beans

1 T. vegetable oil
2 oz. almonds, sliced
3/4 c. green beans, sliced

Heat frying pan over low flame. Add oil and let heat. Add almonds and sauté them gently (be careful not to burn them). Add beans and increase heat to medium flame. Toss beans and almonds together for about 1 minute—long enough for veggies to heat, but not long enough for almonds to burn.

Don Jacobson, *The One Pan Gourmet*

SAUCES AND MIXTURES

Pesto

3 c. (tightly packed) fresh basil leaves, torn in pieces
$1/2$ c. chopped walnuts
3 cloves garlic, minced
$1/2$ t. salt
$3/4$ c. grated Parmesan cheese
$1/2$ c. chopped parsley
plenty of ground black pepper
2 T. olive oil
$1/2$ c. water

You can buy dried pesto, but homemade, as usual, is better. The tough part is blending all the dry ingredients into a paste. A food processor works best, but a blender will do. Mix all dry ingredients and blend slowly into a coarse paste (a little water may be required). Spread on trays and dry gently (125°F or so) until crumbly. Powder thoroughly in a blender.

In the field, mix water into the dried pesto in small dribbles, up to $1/2$ cup, and let stand several minutes. Just before serving, mix in the olive oil. Makes enough pesto to season two generous dinners for two.

Variations:

- try almonds, cashews, or pine nuts instead of walnuts
- cilantro mixed with the parsley makes for a distinctive taste variation

Alan Kesselheim, *Trail Food*

Italian Tomato Sauce

1 medium onion, finely chopped
2 T. olive oil
2 t. dried basil, crumbled
1 t. dried oregano, crumbled
2 T. tomato paste
1 can (28 oz.) crushed tomatoes
salt and pepper to taste

Sauté onion in olive oil until soft. Add all the remaining ingredients and simmer until the sauce is very thick—about 30 minutes. Makes $2^{1}/_2$ cups.

Kay Pastorius, *Cruising Cuisine*

All-Around Tomato Sauce

3 T. olive oil
1 large onion, chopped
3 cloves fresh garlic, minced
1 large green pepper
2 t. basil
1 t. oregano
1 bay leaf
2 t. salt

2 cans (15 oz. ea.) tomato sauce
1 can (6 oz.) tomato paste
1 T. red wine
2 fresh tomatoes, chopped
$1/2$ t. black pepper

Sauté the first group of ingredients. Add the second group and simmer over low heat for an hour or more. Spread on solid trays (puree first, if you like), and dry at 135°F until crisp. Peel off, break up in small pieces, or powder in a blender. Makes enough sauce for two dinners (spaghetti, pizza, etc.).

Variations:

* at the end of cooking, add a handful of chopped parsley

* use additional veggies in initial sauté (mushroom, celery, carrot)

* add ground beef or $1/2$ lb. cubed tofu to the first sauté

Alan Kesselheim, *Trail Food*

Dried Veggie Mix

Many recipes call for a variety of vegetables. Lentil stew, curried rice and vegetables, chili, and soups are all good with a medley of assorted produce. Over the months before a trip I dry everything from asparagus to zucchini. I store each in its own little bag. When I get a good variety and quantity, I dump it all in a bucket and mix it together. Then I scoop 1-cup amounts back into the bags and have ready-mixed vegetable collages, each one unique and primed for the backcountry stew pot.

Alan Kesselheim, *Trail Food*

Hope for good weather at camp, but plan for anything. Sometimes, storm clouds gather so fast, you hardly have time to put up a tarp, never mind fix a warm meal. Or the day's adventure has you famished but so weary you actually consider hitting the sack with only a hastily munched granola bar in your stomach. It's a long way until breakfast, so that homemade dehydrated insta-meal you packed is looking like the better option—it'll be hot and fortifying in only 15 minutes, and you'll be drifting off into sated, restful bliss in no time.

SOMETIMES YOU NEED A HOT MEAL at camp, and you need it quickly. In those cases, dawdling over the dinner pot can be either difficult or dangerous. When light is short, a storm is approaching, or fatigue is overwhelming, try one of these entrées, any one of which can be served up in fifteen minutes. Always plan at least one quick meal for any trip: you never know when you'll be gastronomically grateful for a meal that does away with niceties in exchange for hot fuel in a hurry. Most of these meals have the added advantage of being both compact and lightweight.

HOME-COOKED MEALS RECONSTITUTED

Drying leftovers of your favorite home-cooked chili, beef stew, or spaghetti sauce is easy with a home food dehydrator (see pages 13–16). In the field, all you have to do is simmer in water until the ingredients absorb the liquid and puff up, and you're eating quick meals just as you would at home. Remember that dehydrated foods don't return to their original size even when fully rehydrated, so err on the generous side when you figure portions.

MEATS

Quesadilla Pizza

2 T. vegetable oil
1 pkg. thick flour tortillas (10–12)
1 lb. Cheddar cheese (or other preferred variety), sliced thin
1 pkg. pepperoni slices
additional toppings: tomato slices, olives, artichoke hearts,
    broccoli, etc.

Heat small amount of oil in skillet and warm tortilla on one side, then turn over. Add cheese, pepperoni, and other toppings, then cover pan. Heat over low flame until cheese melts. You're in production: keep cooking and handing them out. Serves 5.

Tasty Chicken Salad

2 T. honey
2 T. vegetable oil
juice of 1 lemon
1/4 t. onion salt (optional)
1 stalk celery, diced
3 deli packets mustard (1 1/2 t.)
1/2 lb. chicken, cooked and diced
1 c. chop suey noodles

In pot, whisk all ingredients except chicken and noodles. Add chicken and noodles and toss to coat.

Don Jacobson, *The One Pan Gourmet*

Chili Rice

1 lb. ground beef
1 envelope chili mix
1 1/3 c. cooked rice
1 can tomato sauce
3 c. water

Brown ground beef. Drain fat. Add remaining ingredients and bring to boil, reduce heat, and simmer 10 minutes. Serves 3–4.

Harriett Barker, *The One-Burner Gourmet*

15-Minute Stroganoff

1 envelope sour cream mix (see page 106)
1 lb. ground beef
1 can (3 oz.) mushroom pieces, drained (reserve liquid)
2/3 c. water
2 T. flour
1 envelope dry onion soup

Prepare sour cream mix and set aside.

Brown meat with mushrooms. Add water and mushroom liquid. Add flour to onion soup mix envelope and stir to combine. Add to meat mixture. Cook until sauce thickens, and simmer a few minutes. Add sour cream and stir.

Serve over cooked rice, cooked noodles, or packaged mashed potatoes. Serves 2–3.

Chef's secret: substitute a can of beef slices in gravy for hamburger.

Harriett Barker, *The One-Burner Gourmet*

VEGGIES

Tostada Night

    1 pkg. tostadas (12)
    2 cans (16 oz. ea.) refried beans
    1 small head lettuce (or 1 bag prepared)
    1 onion, diced
    1 c. salsa
    1 lb. shredded Cheddar cheese
    1 can medium black olives, sliced
    3 tomatoes, chopped
    1 can (4 oz.) chopped green chilis (optional)

A great warm-weather or trailhead meal. Eat cold—just lay
all the ingredients out in an assembly line, pile stuff onto the
tostadas, and that's dinner. Add some warmth—heat refried beans
with some onion, salsa, and green chilis, and then pile everything
on. Serves 5.

Ramen Stew

    3 c. water
    1 pkg. Ramen noodle soup mix and spice packet
       (any flavor)
    1 onion, chopped
    1 red or green pepper, chopped
    1 clove garlic, minced

Bring water to boil. Throw in remaining ingredients. Cook 5
minutes. Serves 1–2.

Couscous Stir Fry

2 c. water
1 c. couscous
1 T. olive oil
1 onion, diced
1 clove garlic, minced
1 red pepper, cut in strips
1 c. shredded or chopped cabbage
1 pkg. dried stir-fry sauce

Bring water to a boil and add couscous. Cover and remove from heat. In skillet, heat oil, then sauté onion, garlic, pepper, and cabbage until just tender. Add stir-fry sauce. Serve sautéed vegetables and sauce over the couscous. Serves 2.

Bleu Cheese Walnut Salad

1 c. broken walnut pieces
1 bunch leaf lettuce, torn
1 Granny Smith apple, chopped
4 oz. bleu cheese, crumbled
1 c. Dijon-type vinaigrette

Toast walnuts for 10 minutes in Dutch oven or in 350°F conventional oven. Toss the lettuce with nuts and remaining ingredients. Makes 6 servings.

Sheila Mills, *The Outdoor Dutch Oven Cookbook*

A good cup o' Joe or your afternoon "cuppa tea"—they rev you up for a new day, relax you before bedtime, let you touch base with routine—just for a moment—before the adventure continues. And that's when a sweet treat appears, proving you wrong when you thought dinner couldn't have been better.

A DESSERT FOLLOWING DINNER, a cup of tea before bed, a good cup of coffee to start the day . . . food around the fringes of the main gastronomic events of a journey. No less important for being on the edges of the food scene, however. An occasional dessert, and a selection of drinks to lubricate the trip gears, qualify as critical intangibles in the quest for expedition culinary greatness. Don't neglect the fringes of the food experience. You and your companions will be happier and better company for it.

HOT DRINKS

A WORD ABOUT HOT DRINKS

Hot drinks fall into one of those common-sense categories that almost any camp cook can manage. Consider a few suggestions, however, beyond the usual tea, cocoa, and coffee trio.

- try hot Tang or lemonade crystals for a sweet variation
- add lemonade crystals to your tea
- bouillon, miso soup mix, or Cup o' Soup can be restorative on a drizzly, cold afternoon
- if you can't stomach dried milk or nondairy creamer, pack a small can of evaporated milk to add to your coffee or tea

A WORD ABOUT COFFEE

Coffee is in a hot-drink category by itself. The New Age java craze has arrived in the backcountry in the guise of compact, stove-top espresso units, cappuccino condiment dispensers, coffee bags (similar to tea bags), hand-crank coffee bean grinders, and more.

My current favorite coffee gadget is a press pot inside a tough, metal thermos. It makes great coffee, but it's an expensive toy and bulky for backpacking.

When all the geegaws and gizmos are stripped away, what we are left with is good old chuckwagon cowboy coffee. There is much debate over the proper way to handle a pot of cowboy mud and the best way to stop the rolling action and settle the grounds when the brew is done. I've witnessed strategies that run the gamut from dropping a raw egg into the pot to employing centrifugal force by winging the pot in high-speed, full-circle arm rotations. It doesn't have to be that complicated. Here's my time-tested recipe.

Put 2 quarts cold water in a pot and add about five handfuls of fresh coffee grounds (this is an inexact science, remember). Bring to a brisk boil, then remove from the heat. If you have a few minutes, let the grounds settle on their own. A couple of sharp taps with a spoon on the side of the pot will settle the last few. If you're in a rush, add $1/2$ cup cold water to settle the grounds, then pour.

Hot Chocolate

1 c. dried milk
$1/2$ c. coffee lightener
$1/4$ c. cocoa
4 T. sugar
$1/8$ t. salt
3 c. water

At home, combine all dry ingredients thoroughly in a sturdy plastic bag.

At camp, pour the contents of the bag into a pot. Add water, stir with a wire whip, and heat just to boiling. Turn heat very low and keep cocoa warm for a few minutes to blend flavors before serving. Makes about 4 cups.

Chef's secret: Add $1/2$ teaspoon molasses to coffee or hot chocolate for a new taste.

Harriett Barker, *The One-Burner Gourmet*

Here's to great trip food!

DESSERTS

Sweet Torts

1 T. butter or margarine
$1/2$ c. brown sugar
1 t. cinnamon
dash of nutmeg
10–12 corn or flour tortillas
1 c. dried berries

Melt fat in a frying pan at medium heat. Mix sugar, cinnamon, and nutmeg in a cup. Quickly brown one side of a tortilla in butter, then flip it over. Sprinkle sugar and spice mixture across the top of the tortilla, cover pan, and heat until the tort is crisp and the sugar has melted somewhat. Sprinkle berries (either dried or rehydrated) atop the baked tortillas.

Alan Kesselheim, *Trail Food*

S'mores

graham crackers
chocolate bars, broken into squares
marshmallows

This is the all-time favorite camping dessert. Break a cracker in half and place a chocolate square on one half.

Toast a marshmallow over the campfire or grill fire until golden brown (or darker, as you prefer).

Place it on the chocolate, top with the other half of cracker, and gently press it all together.

Variation: Tired of the same ol', same ol'? Try using the following.

- peanut butter or toasted peanuts instead of chocolate to make Robinson Crusoes
- slices of apple instead of crackers to make Apple S'mores
- chocolate-covered graham crackers and omit chocolate bars
- chocolate peppermint patties instead of chocolate bars

Victoria Logue, Frank Logue, and Mark Carroll, *Kids Outdoors*

Better than S'mores

1 ripe banana
1 small milk chocolate bar
12 miniature marshmallows

On the concave side of each banana, peel back one-third of the skin, leaving it attached at the stem end. Using the tip of spoon, make a pocket in the banana for stuffing by scooping out about a quarter of the pulp.

Place chocolate in the indentation and top with marshmallows. Fold banana skin back in place and wrap tightly in aluminum foil that has been sprayed with a nonstick coating.

If not barbecuing, bake the bananas in a 375°F oven 15 minutes. Allow to cool slightly before unwrapping. Makes 1 serving.

Kay Pastorius, *Cruising Cuisine*

Blind Dates

12 pitted dates
3 oz. cream cheese
12 pecans

Cut dates in half lengthwise, spoon a dollop of cream cheese (about 1 tablespoon) into the cavity, and settle a pecan firmly on top.

Alan Kesselheim, *Trail Food*

Coconuts to You Fruit Cup

1 orange, peeled and cubed
1 apple or pear, cubed
1 banana, peeled and sliced (optional)
1/4 c. shredded coconut
1 T. sugar (optional)

Mix all ingredients (sugar is optional) together and let stand in a covered dish for 30 minutes. Eat with great joy.

Don Jacobson, *The One Pan Gourmet*

Apple Delight

2 McIntosh apples, top half peeled
2 T. raisins
1 T. sugar
cinnamon to taste

Core apples without puncturing bottoms. In bowl, mix sugar and raisins. Stuff each apple with raisin-sugar mixture. Sprinkle cinnamon over top. Pour enough water in pot to reach bottom of steamer. Place apples on steamer.

Place steamer in pot. Cover pot and cook over medium flame. Allow to steam at least 30 minutes, adding water if needed.

Don Jacobson, *The One Pan Gourmet*

Apple Cinnamon Brown Betty

$1/2$ lb. (2 sticks) unsalted butter, melted (plus enough
    to grease Dutch oven)
2 c. rolled oats
2 c. unbleached all-purpose flour
2 c. brown sugar
2 t. ground cinnamon
$1/2$ t. baking powder
2 T. cornstarch
5 T. fresh lemon juice (about 2 large lemons)
6 c. apples, peeled and sliced

Grease a 12-inch Dutch oven or 9-by-13-inch baking pan and set aside.

Mix butter, oats, flour, brown sugar, cinnamon, and baking powder. Set aside.

In a separate large bowl, mix cornstarch and lemon juice. Add apples and toss to coat with juice mixture. Sprinkle one third the oatmeal mixture over the bottom of Dutch oven or baking pan. Spread apple mixture in an even layer on top. Sprinkle remaining oatmeal mixture evenly over apples.

Bake in Dutch oven about 30 minutes, or in 350°F conventional oven about 35–40 minutes, until topping is light golden brown. Cut into squares and serve warm.

Makes 12 servings.

Sheila Mills, *The Outdoor Dutch Oven Cookbook*

Blueberry Cobbler

Filling:
4 c. fresh blueberries
5 T. sugar
3/4 c. orange juice

Topping:
1 c. unbleached all-purpose flour
1/2 t. baking powder
1/8 t. salt
1/2 lb. (2 sticks) butter, softened
1 c. sugar
1 egg
1/2 t. vanilla extract

Make filling: mix blueberries, sugar, and orange juice. Pour into a 12-inch Dutch oven or 9-by-13-inch baking pan.

Make the topping: Mix flour, baking powder, and salt in a small bowl and set aside. Mix butter and sugar until well blended. Stir in egg and vanilla, then stir in flour mixture. Drop topping by tablespoonfuls on blueberry mixture.

Bake in Dutch oven 30–40 minutes, or in 350°F conventional oven 40–45 minutes, until cobbler topping is golden brown and filling is bubbly. Cool slightly before serving.

Makes 8–10 servings.

Sheila Mills, *The Outdoor Dutch Oven Cookbook*

Apple Heaven

2 medium apples (McIntosh are best), sliced thin
2 T. brown sugar
1/2 t. cinnamon
1/2 t. nutmeg
2 t. margarine

Place apples in oven pan. Sprinkle with brown sugar and spices and dot with margarine. Cover and bake in medium oven 20 minutes.

Don Jacobson, *The One Pan Gourmet*

Apple Crisp

Crust:
3 c. quick oats
2 c. brown sugar
1 c. unbleached all-purpose flour
1 t. baking soda
2 t. salt
1 c. melted butter (plus enough butter to grease Dutch oven)

Filling:
6–8 apples, peeled, cored, and thinly sliced
2 t. cinnamon
2 t. nutmeg

Butter Dutch oven or 9-by-12-inch baking pan.

Mix together well the oats, brown sugar, flour, baking soda, and salt. Add melted butter and combine.

Cover bottom of Dutch oven or pan with half the crust mixture.

Mix apples with cinnamon and nutmeg. Layer in Dutch oven or pan about 2 inches thick over bottom crust. Spread remaining crust mixture on top.

With coals on top of and beneath Dutch oven (see page 22), bake 40–50 minutes. For conventional cooking, bake in 350°F oven 40–50 minutes. Makes 8–10 servings.

Sheila Mills, *The Outdoor Dutch Oven Cookbook*

Sue's Apple Raisin Crumble

Filling:
6 large apples, peeled and sliced
$1/2$ c. raisins
$1/2$ c. honey
1 t. ground cinnamon

Crumble Crust:
$1^1/2$ c. quick oats, uncooked
1 T. sesame seeds
1 T. wheat germ
$1/4$ c. coconut
$1/4$ c. sunflower seeds
$1/2$ c. margarine (plus enough to grease Dutch oven)
$1/2$ c. honey

Grease a Dutch oven or 9-by-12-inch baking pan and set aside.

Make filling: mix apples, raisins, honey, and cinnamon. Pour into Dutch oven or pan and set aside.

Make crust: Mix oats, sesame seeds, wheat germ, coconut, and sunflower seeds. Cut in margarine and add enough honey to create a crumbly texture. Cover the filling with the crumble mixture.

Bake 30 minutes in Dutch oven, or for 30 minutes in 350°F conventional oven, until top is golden brown. Makes 8 servings.

Sheila Mills, *The Outdoor Dutch Oven Cookbook*

War Cake

- 2 c. water
- 2 c. sugar
- 1 c. shortening (plus enough to grease Dutch oven)
- 2 c. raisins
- 1 c. walnuts, optional
- 1/2 t. ground cloves
- 1 t. ground cinnamon
- 2 c. unbleached all-purpose flour (approximate; plus enough to dust Dutch oven)
- 1/4 t. allspice
- 2 t. baking soda

This recipe doesn't call for eggs, butter, or milk, which explains its name. Grease and flour a Dutch oven or 9-by-12-inch cake pan and set aside.

Combine water, sugar, shortening, raisins, walnuts (if desired), cloves, and cinnamon in a saucepan and bring to a boil. Allow mixture to cool, then add enough flour to stiffen. Mix in allspice and baking soda.

Bake in Dutch oven 30 minutes, or in 325°F conventional oven 30 minutes, or until center springs back when touched. Makes 12 servings.

Sheila Mills, *The Outdoor Dutch Oven Cookbook*

Dutch Oven Kuchen

3 c. white flour
1 1/2 c. brown sugar
1 t. baking powder
1/2 t. salt
1/2 c. oil
1 1/3 c. milk
2 dried eggs (see recipe page 16), rehydrated
    in 1/2 c. water
2 t. vanilla
1 t. nutmeg
dried lemon peel
2 c. dried fruit (berries are good)
1/4 c. brown sugar

Mix together the first four ingredients. Add oil, milk, and eggs all at once and mix again. Add vanilla, nutmeg, and lemon peel and stir once more. Finally, stir in dried fruit and brown sugar.

Spread in oiled 10- or 12-inch Dutch oven and bake under coals until that smell wafts up and it's browned just right (30–40 minutes). This is best hot but can also be baked the night before.

Alan Kesselheim, *Trail Food*

Conversions and Equivalents

TEMPERATURE

°F	°C
175	80
200	95
225	105
250	120
275	135
300	150
325	165
350	175
375	185
400	205
425	220
450	230
475	245

slow oven = 300–325°F (150–165°C)
medium oven = 350–375°F (175–185°C)
hot oven = 400–425°F (205–220°C)

For other conversions:
$$(°F − 32) × 0.555 = °C$$
$$(°C × 1.8) + 32 = °F$$

WEIGHT

1 ounce (oz.) = 28.35 grams (g)
1 pound (lb.) = 16 ounces = 453.6 grams (g)
2.2 pounds (lb.) = 1 kilogram (kg)

(continued next page)

VOLUME

1 teaspoon (t.) = 5 milliliters (mL)

1 tablespoon (T.) = 3 teaspoons (t.) = 15 milliliters (mL)

1 teaspoon (t.) = 4 milliliters (mL)

1 fluid ounce (oz.) = 6 teaspoons (t.) = 1/8 cup (c.)
$\qquad$ = 29.56 milliliters (mL)

1 cup = 16 tablespoons (T.) = 8 fluid ounces (oz.)
$\qquad$ = 236 milliliters (mL)

1 pint (pt.) = 16 fluid ounces (oz.) = 2 cups (c.) = 0.5 liter (L)

1 quart (qt.) = 32 fluid ounces (oz.) = 2 pints (pt.) = 0.9 liter (L)

1 gallon (gal.) = 64 fluid ounces (oz.) = 4 quarts (qt.)
$\qquad$ = 3.8 liters (L)

LENGTH

1 inch (in.) = 2.54 centimeters (cm)

Acknowledgments

My recipe thievery was made possible by the generous permission granted by a handful of authors and publishers. And my culinary range has grown by a quantum leap as a result. Thanks to all.

Recipes attributed to the following books are reprinted with the permission of the author or publisher:

Harriett Barker, *The One-Burner Gourmet* (Chicago: Contemporary, 1981).

Garrett Conover and Alexandra Conover, *The Winter Wilderness Companion: Traditional and Native American Skills for the Undiscovered Season* (Camden ME: Ragged Mountain Press, 2001).

Don Jacobson, *The One Pan Gourmet: Fresh Food on the Trail* (Camden ME: Ragged Mountain Press, 1993).

Alan S. Kesselheim, *Trail Food: Drying and Cooking Food for Backpackers and Paddlers* (Camden ME: Ragged Mountain Press, 1998).

Victoria Logue, Frank Logue, and Mark Carroll, *Kids Outdoors: Skills and Knowledge for Outdoor Adventurers* (Camden ME: Ragged Mountain Press, 1996).

Sheila Mills, *The Outdoor Dutch Oven Cookbook* (Camden ME: Ragged Mountain Press, 1997).

Kay Pastorius, *Cruising Cuisine: Fresh Food from the Galley* (Camden ME: International Marine, 1997).

Jean and Samuel Spangenberg, *The Portable Baker: Baking on Boat and Trail* (Camden ME: Ragged Mountain Press, 1997).

Index

Numbers in **bold** refer to pages with illustrations